Trading Freedom

How Free Trade Affects Our Lives, Work, and Environment

Edited by
John Cavanagh, John Gershman,
Karen Baker and Gretchen Helmke

A Food First Book
in association with the
Institute for Policy Studies

The Institute for Food and Development Policy
San Francisco

Institute for Food and Development Policy
145 Ninth Street
San Francisco, California 94103

Library of Congress Cataloging-in-Publication Data

Trading Freedom: how free trade affects our lives, work and
    environment / edited by John Cavanagh ... [et al.]. --1st ed.
    p. cm.
    "A Food First book in association with the Institute for Policy Studies."
    Includes bibliographical references.
    ISBN 0-935028-59-5
    1. Free trade – United States. 2. Free trade – Canada. 3. Free trade – Mexico. 4.
United States – Commerce – Canada. 5. Canada – Commerce – United States. 6.
United Sates – Commerce – Mexico. 7. Mexico – Commerce – United States. I
Cavanagh, John. II. Institute for Food and Development Policy (San Francisco,
Calif.) III. Institute for Policy Studies.
    HF1455.T674 1992   91-37605
    382'.71'097--dc20   CIP
                                                          r91

Book Design by Ian McWilliam
Typeset in Frutiger and ITC Stone
Printed on recycled paper by Capital City Press, Montpelier, Vermont, USA
First Edition January 1992

® GCIU ⊷

Contents

Acknowledgments

This book is a genuinely collective work. While it represents the collaborative efforts of two institutions on opposite ends of the United States, it also reflects the results of many organizations and individuals throughout North America working to build a democratic, equitable, and sustainable future for the peoples of North America. The editors have been the beneficiaries of this experience and expertise, for these people have been invaluable partners in this project. While many people in three countries helped to put this book together, we would like to thank in particular Adolfo Aguilar Zinser, David Brooks, Tony Clarke, Jon Fox, and Mary McGinn for their helpful comments, advice, and support.

John Gershman and Gretchen Helmke of the Institute for Food and Development Policy would like to thank Marilyn Borchardt, Denise Newman, Sanae Miyaji, Kristen Wiegers, Stephanie Rosenfeld, Walden Bello, Martha Katigbak, and Ian McWilliam, for great suggestions and a valuable sense of humor. John Cavanagh and Karen Baker of the Institute for Policy Studies would like to thank their colleagues for their support and encouragement on this project. Richard Barnet and Peter Andreas helped them think through the implications of free trade in the age of globalization; Richard Healey encouraged the international collaboration; and Carolyn Bancroft helped on several aspects of the book. The four editors offer this book as an example of what international collaboration at its best can produce and we encourage more joint ventures of this nature in the future.

We salute the *Trabajadores Desplazados*, the workers at Ford's plant in Cuautitlán, Mexico, the Cree and Inuit peoples of James Bay and the many other individuals and organizations whose sacrifices and struggles for a new North America inspired this book. The editors dedicate this book to David Hunter in recognition of his support and commitment to Food First and the Institute for Policy Studies.

Foreword

Free Trade as Opportunity
John Cavanagh

George Herbert Walker Bush made this book both possible and necessary. Within a three-week period in June 1990, he launched two initiatives that lay out some of the most profound choices that confront the 700 million people of the Western Hemisphere – including the 250 million who call the US home – in this final decade of the twentieth century.

The first was a proposal for a US-Mexico free trade agreement, which has since turned into tri-national negotiations among the US, Mexico and Canada for a North American Free Trade Agreement. The second was immodestly called the 'Enterprise for the Americas' and it presented a vision of uniting the entire hemisphere "from the port of Anchorage to Tierra del Fuego" in a massive free trade pact that would surpass anything the world has yet seen.

In these two initiatives, the Bush Administration laid down an economic agenda for its new world order. The agenda is, upon closer examination, one that should prove enormously lucrative to a few thousand very large corporations, amounting to what Maude Barlow of the Council of Canadians calls "a corporate bill of rights." It would commit the hemisphere to a path where the economic destiny of communities, regions, and entire nations is increasingly decided in boardrooms of global corporations, largely unaccountable to the public and unfettered by government regulation. Trade and investment patterns of these firms will increasingly shape the development paths of the three countries instead of serving the development needs of their communities.

Many in the hemisphere are letting it be known that they think that Bush has set forth the wrong agenda. Hence we are in for a series of big battles that have begun with the North America free trade proposals and that, as the decade progresses, will spread to the entire hemisphere. Part of the battles will be at the level of rhetoric, with George Bush and the Fortune 500 promising to harvest the fruits of globalization, to enhance our competitiveness *vis-à-vis* Japan and Europe, and to deliver progress and prosperity. Another front on which the battles will be waged is that of statistics, with the free trade advocates promising new jobs, a massive expansion of trade, and the economic growth which they posit comes with both.

Citizens of all nations must wade into these muddied waters. We must confront the rhetoric and examine the assumptions that underlie it. We must challenge their statistics and generate our own. But most of all, we must reshape the terms of the debate to the issue of who should have the right to determine the social and economic future of our communities, our nations and, ultimately, our hemisphere. Through the international citizens' dialogues that are already underway, we must lay out an alternative agenda wherein connections between our peoples and our economies enhance basic human rights, the long-term sustainable use of our natural resources, and the economic viability of our communities. We must challenge the promoters of free trade at each stage and we must, at the same time, offer viable alternatives.

The first steps in this direction have already been taken. Since the fall of 1990, citizens groups across the US and Mexico have come together to address the free trade issue in this hemisphere, linking up with Canadian groups that have been mobilizing effectively around the issue for half a decade. In less than a year, these groups were able to achieve some impressive gains:

- The media now regularly reports on the opposition in coverage of the US-Mexico-Canada agreement.
- The Bush Administration has had to back-pedal on early statements that the proposed agreement would not touch on key issues such as environmental standards and labor rights. It is already offering some concessions on these issues.
- US labor, environmental, and consumer groups are working with religious and agricultural communities to address fundamental questions raised by this debate, including the issue of what kind of development path the US should pursue.

If we are to build on these initial steps, we must understand that this is a long struggle and that we may lose some early battles. The free trade advocates have the power of enormous financial resources on their side, resources they deployed liberally in the first round of the free trade fight in the form of millions of dollars for lobbyists and public relations. Thus we can prevail only if we muster the power of sheer numbers, since the proposed free trade framework is likely to harm far more people than it will benefit. To expand our numbers, we must begin by exposing what the Bush free trade agenda is and what is behind the lofty rhetoric used to sell it.

The Bush Agenda

Bush's free trade vision is being advanced on three fronts: North America, the Western Hemisphere, and the globe.

North America: The proposed free trade agreement among the US, Mexico and Canada would lower barriers to goods flowing between the North American countries and remove most barriers that deter corporations in one country from investing in another. Given comparatively low wages and lax enforcement of environmental standards in Mexico, such an agreement would accelerate the shift of US and Canadian factories to Mexico. In May of 1991, the US Congress voted to renew Bush's authority to negotiate this (and other) trade agreements on a 'fast-track' basis, which eliminates Congress' ability to amend any agreement that Bush brings before them.

Western Hemisphere: Under the rubric of a grand 'Enterprise for the Americas,' Bush is laying the groundwork for a free trade area to cover the entire hemisphere through two sets of negotiations. The first is a series of 'bilateral framework agreements' with individual nations that lay out a framework for the lowering of trade and investment barriers. By the first anniversary of Bush's June 1990 'Enterprise' speech, fifteen such agreements had been signed.

The second set of negotiations is creating regional frameworks for reducing trade and investment barriers. As of July 1991, agreements had been signed with the four nations of the southern cone of Latin America and with the 13 English-speaking nations of the Caribbean; talks were underway with the nations of Central America and the Andean region. Bush sees all these adding up to a new Common Market of the Americas within a decade. The 'Enterprise' initiative also includes a small plan for heavily conditioned debt relief and a new investment fund.

The Globe: The first two fronts of Bush's trade offensive supplement an ongoing effort to reduce global trade barriers under the auspices of the intergovernmental General Agreement on Tariffs and Trade (GATT). Since the end of World War II, this body has met in marathon trade rounds that last several years, and it has succeeded in reducing tariff barriers to trade in much of the world. The current round, dubbed the Uruguay Round, is coming to an end after a major effort by the US to expand GATT's domain beyond trade in goods to address lowering barriers to foreign investment in services like banking and insurance. A major dispute between the US and Europe over the latter's heavily subsidized agricultural sector, which the US government views as an unfair barrier to trade, threatens to kill the trade round altogether (see articles by Martin Khor and Robert Schaeffer).

On all three negotiating fronts, the Bush Administration is attempting to remove the barriers that governments have erected to protect certain areas of their economy from foreign corporate intrusions. In the stark imagery of US Treasury Under-Secretary David Mulford: "The countries that do not make themselves attractive will not get investors' attention ... This is like a girl trying to get a boyfriend. She has to go out, have her hair done up, wear make up." [1]

The Administration is also using the carrot of greater access to the US market to push countries to accept the Reaganomic goal of getting the government out of the economy by privatizing state-owned enterprises and cutting government spending. US Assistant Secretary of State Bernard Aronson calls this "an economic revolution of equally far-reaching consequence" to the "political revolution throughout the Americas" of the last decade that buried "a tradition of dictatorship through the peaceful act of going to the polls." [2]

Bush's primary motivation for launching the two initiatives in this hemisphere in 1990 appears to have been his fear that Japan's surging economic strength and Europe's 1992 economic unification were leaving the US in their economic wake. Indeed, Europe's unification drive was already attracting a great deal of investment – including US corporations – into that region. By holding out the prospect of a unified Western hemispheric market of 700 million people, Bush hopes to attract investors away from the 360 million-strong European pact. The two initiatives also serve as an insurance policy that Bush's free trade agenda could advance even should the global GATT talks founder.

Key Terms

Coming to grips with free trade requires making sense of three terms that are bandied about quite carelessly in the public debate: globalization, competitiveness, and sovereignty.

Globalization: Few would contest that we have entered the 'age of globalization' – although the phrase can mean whatever its user wants it to mean. Bush and other administration officials present free trade agreements as stepping stones toward a global village in which everyone benefits: workers will have more jobs in global factories, and consumers will have a smorgasbord of global choices in global shopping centers.

Yet a key problem with the globalization that the Bush Administration is energetically promoting through 'free trade' is precisely that not everyone is invited in. How many can afford the mangoes, star apples and kiwi fruits that now add color to Safeway's grocery sections? Indeed, pockets of the US and Canada and the majority in Mexico and the other nations to the south of us are simply too poor to buy the new goods that will be available in their expanding malls. The shifting of jobs to spots where wages are lowest will only deepen the division between the haves and the have nots. And, the incentive to local and national governments to ignore environmental standards in order to attract new investment augurs a global environmental disaster. In short: beware the promises of globalization.

Competitiveness: In the name of staying competitive with the Japanese and Europeans, free trade advocates can justify almost anything. In the plush bar of Washington, DC's Ritz Carlton Hotel, Mexico's articulate Commerce Minister Jaime Serra Puche tried to sell a new free trade agreement to me as a marriage of Mexico's inexpensive labor with the US' high-skilled workforce. The ensuing union, he argued, could beat back the Japanese and Koreans on world markets.

The catch here is that the logic of competing globally in a free market suggests that one must lower production costs to the least common global denominator. In order to underprice a high quality sweater produced by repressed Korean workers, one must likewise compete in exploitation. Put another way, in the age of extremely mobile global corporations, cars, VCRs, and most other products can be produced almost anywhere. Countries gain advantage mainly by producing things more cheaply than their neighbors, which can be done by allowing corporations to exploit workers and to ignore costly environmental, health, and safety standards.

The only possible counter to this logic in an increasingly integrated global market is the creation of strict and enforceable international norms that protect worker rights and environmental standards. The competitiveness argument sets us all on a course of downwardly spiralling wages, working conditions and standards. One of the central challenges in the age of globalization is to determine the international norms that should accompany trade agreements, so that trade reinforces basic rights and levels standards in an upward direction.

One other aspect of the competitiveness issue that is particularly ironic is that since Bush launched the idea of North American free trade, Taiwanese, Korean and Japanese firms have been rushing into Mexico to make everything from baseball caps to toys to furniture to bicycles. Nissan is already the largest car maker in Mexico and around 100 Japanese, Korean and Taiwanese plants are producing consumer electronics in the border region with the US. It is hard to compete with East Asian manufacturers when they are increasingly part of you.

Sovereignty: National sovereignty is an especially confusing concept in an age where corporations move goods and capital across borders almost at will, where pollution and disease roam around the planet with ease, and where in many parts of the world strong regional identities threaten to break apart nations and redefine the global map. Yet, governments still do defend their borders militarily, still offer certain services to their own citizens that they deny to others, and continue to regulate the flow of people in and out of their countries.

Many opponents of the proposed free trade pacts invoke the notion of sovereignty to argue that governments should be able to designate certain industries, services, portions of agriculture, cultural enterprises, and their own natural resources (particularly oil) as off-limits to foreign ownership. This is a difficult argument since there are few countries where governments actually manage these industries and resources in a fashion that redounds to the benefit of the people of that country. Mexican oil, for example, has enriched the few at the expense of the many despite its control by the Mexican government. And with respect to culture, who is willing or able to stop McDonald's, Madonna, and Michael Jackson from entering people's homes?

In the name of sovereignty, however, opponents of the proposed free trade pacts are raising an important issue. They are saying that some things are worth preserving. Local artists outside the US often argue that a share of television time should be devoted to domestically-produced programs.

Similar arguments hold for agriculture. Many Mexicans argue that it is worth protecting the livelihood of the millions of subsistence farmers who would be reduced to wage earners on fruit and vegetable plantations or into urban slum dwellers by a free trade agreement. Many Europeans argue that their governments are justified in spending state revenues to support an agricultural sector that free trade would wipe out. US Trade Representative Carla Hills calls these supports "obsolete" and "wrong."[3] In effect, she wants private corporations unfettered by government supports or restrictions to determine who produces what and where and which countries can have an agricultural sector.

Opponents of free trade do not glorify all agricultural producers everywhere. Keep in mind that large sugar growers in Florida 'employ' Haitian and Dominican workers in slave-like conditions that have changed little from the first Caribbean sugar plantations of five centuries ago. Rather, many of us are saying that decisions about who can produce what should lie with the communities that are affected, as long as basic rights are respected. Thus, 'community sovereignty' might be a better term. Or, perhaps the concept we should be advancing is that of 'self-determination.' The key to genuine democracy in this decade will be the struggle by communities and citizens' organizations to control their own destinies, to take control of their own lands and natural resources, to collectively make the decisions that affect their futures. The free trade agreements that are currently on the table appropriate these decisions and toss them to the private sector.

If the governments and corporations of the Western Hemisphere have a free trade ideology that guides their negotiations, the citizens of these countries have an even more powerful set of principles that can guide our critique and our alternative. There are several documents of the United Nations that spell out a universal notion of the rights that should be at the core of development in any nation. U.N. International Labor Organization conventions, for example, clearly delineate what internationally-recognized worker rights should not be violated in a trade agreement.

Perhaps the most important documents that can offer guidance to our work are the U.N. Universal Declaration on Human Rights and the U.N. Declaration on the Right to Development. As opposed to free traders' narrow focus on economic growth as the ultimate goal, the latter United Nations document recognizes that development must aim "at the constant improvement of the well-being of ... all individuals on the basis of their active, free and meaningful participation in development and in the fair distribution of the benefits resulting therefrom."

A task that is worthy of extended debate is how one can advance the understanding and practice of self-determination at a community level while at the same time fashioning new international norms and conventions that guarantee the basic political, social, economic and cultural rights of all peoples. As we experiment in this direction, be wary of governments that respond to international citizens' attempts to advance worker or other basic rights with the cry: "You are violating our national sovereignty." Basic internationally-recognized human rights transcend national sovereignty.

On these issues, we have much to learn from Western Europe, where similar debates have been waged for over seven years as those nations have worked toward a more unified European free trade arena. Worker and other citizens groups there have put forward a 'social charter' that will be a part of Europe 1992; they have forced the expansion of social and development funds through which billions of dollars go to communities and groups adversely affected by economic integration.[4] The European experience raises the question, do 'social contracts' that temper some of the worst aspects of an agreement principally serve to legitimize freer trade and investment?

The Impact of North American Free Trade

Over the next year, the debate on free trade will be focused primarily on the proposed US-Mexico-Canada free trade agreement. With fast-track authority in hand, Bush has rushed into tri-national negotiations and hopes to have an agreement signed in 1992. Section Two of this book lays out a series of arguments by authors from all three countries as to why the proposed agreement serves the few at the expense of the many. In addition to the basic development issues, the arguments are centered on six areas: jobs, justice, food, freedom, debt, and democracy.

Jobs: Organized labor in the US emphasizes that Mexican wages that hover around 60 cents an hour combined with high productivity levels have attracted close to 2,000 factories employing a half million Mexicans – many of them children – across the border from Texas, Arizona and California. Tens of thousands of US auto, food processing, furniture and other jobs have been lost in the process.

According to Richard Rothstein of the Economic Policy Institute, US corporations also have used the threat of shifting factories abroad to depress US wages by an average of 10 percent over the 1980s. Sweatshop conditions are spreading in an astounding number of US apparel and other industries, particularly in large urban areas, with women and people of color (many recent arrivals from the Third World) bearing the brunt of the exploitation. Even the US government's International Trade Commission admits that this trend is likely to continue. They concluded that unskilled US workers, who make up 70 percent of our workforce, are likely to suffer a decline in income if Bush's version of the agreement with Mexico and Canada is implemented. And, the Mexican jobs that will be created are likely to be at wage rates that do not allow an average family to rise above the poverty level.

Justice: Justice for workers is but one concern of those opposed to a quick agreement with Mexico. A glimpse of the extent to which broader goals of economic, social and environmental justice can be violated with freer trade and investment is provided by those same border factories, also known as *maquiladoras*, where goods are assembled for export to the US. Lack of adequate housing, exposure of workers to dangerous toxic substances, and contamination of drinking water with industrial pollutants have turned the Mexican side of the border into an environmental wasteland and industrial slum. A new free trade agreement could only help spread the slum south and north, farther into the Mexican and US heartlands.

Given the permeability of borders, we have frequently seen the toxic pollutants and untreated sewage from the maquiladoras flow though waterways into the US. Thus, for example, Arizona health officials are reporting hepatitis rates 20 times the national average. Poor enforcement of health and environmental standards on the Mexico side is a strong inducement for US firms to move south. A once-vibrant furniture industry in Southern California has been decimated by US corporations fleeing new US air quality standards; many US factory owners simply shifted production to Mexico (see article by Richard Rothstein).

Presidents Bush and Salinas and Prime Minister Mulroney would prefer to keep health, safety, worker rights, and environmental justice off the trade agenda. Citizens' groups are insisting that binding and enforceable labor and environmental standards be included.

Food: Free trade proponents love to conjure up images of ever-expanding shipments of succulent Mexican strawberries, tomatoes and oranges serving US consumers even in the dead of winter, while Mexicans buy more and more US corn and grains.

Yet, agriculture groups have been among the most vocal opponents of Bush's trade agenda. Some Mexican groups argue that the spread of plantations to grow food for the US, combined with a flood of cheap grain imports from the US, will wipe out millions of small subsistence producers. Likewise, in the US, freer trade is destined to accelerate the demise of small, single-family farms and the consolidation of large plantation-style agriculture employing low-wage labor largely from Latin America and the Caribbean.

These scenarios lead many agricultural groups in both countries to suggest proceeding with caution. Liberalization of trade and investment, they warn, should be done very slowly and carefully, only after extensive national discussions about what kind of agricultural sector each country wants to preserve.

Freedom: To curry favor with the US, the Mexican government has been pursuing a concerted policy of economic liberalization. In addition to lowering barriers to trade and foreign investment, this has included downward pressure on wages and a reduction in government spending on social programs. Proponents of economic liberalization argue that the short-term suffering of the people will be offset by longer-term growth.

In the meantime, social unrest sparked by this liberalization has been met by a persistent increase in human rights abuses in Mexico – from torture in prisons to election fraud to harassment of vocal opponents of free trade. Likewise, abuses by US border officials of the growing numbers of Mexican workers who seek to escape the grinding poverty of their country are rampant. Citizen groups want better human rights monitoring to be part of the negotiations.

Debt: By focusing the free trade agenda exclusively on trade and investment, Bush has purposefully left off the bargaining table what many believe is the largest single impediment to Mexican development: a $90 billion external debt which sucks vast amounts of foreign exchange out of the country each year – $9 billion in 1990 – to repay creditor banks. Many Mexicans and growing numbers in Canada and the US believe that substantial debt reduction in Mexico could provide a far greater impetus to its development than a further freeing up of trade and investment.

Democracy: Thus far, communities, workers and consumers have effectively been left out of shaping the 'free trade' component of Bush's new world order. Now, however, citizens' organizations are demanding to be part of the discussion. If democracy is to have meaning, discussions on the integration of our nations should include those whose lives will be most affected.

The Challenge

Unwittingly, George Bush has offered the citizens' movements of the Western Hemisphere a tremendous opportunity. By unveiling an agenda that will occupy the governments of our nations with negotiations for the next decade, he has given us a framework for hemispheric partnership. Over the next year, the emphasis of necessity will be on US-Mexico-Canada dialogues, an arena where groups like the *Mexico-US Diálogos* have already begun to build relations of trust. These dialogues should prove an educational bonanza for groups in the US. For close to a half decade, Canadian groups have mobilized against the free trade agenda; they have excellent education materials and a long history of articulating what kind of development is good for Canadians. With one-ninth the population of the US, they offer a microcosm of what might work in the US.

Mexico likewise has a mobilized opposition with enormous energy and new ideas. Indeed, the Mexican opposition has laid out a vision for a continental alternative to free trade that can serve as a starting point for trinational citizens discussions. In a speech in early 1991, Mexican opposition leader Cuauhtémoc Cárdenas identified a key issue in his criticism of the Bush agenda for free trade: "Economic liberalization is not our objective, it is one of our tools. Development, social justice and a clean environment are our objectives."

Exciting initiatives are likewise underway in the US. The Mobilization on Development, Trade, Labor and the Environment (MODTLE) has unified religious, farm, consumer, labor and environmental groups to fight free trade and advance alternatives. The Coalition for Justice in the Maquiladoras has spelled out a corporate code of conduct for firms on the US-Mexican border, and is mobilizing groups to hold these firms accountable.

Let us view this next period as one of discussion, debate, and experimentation at community, national, and regional levels. We can learn a great deal by simply sharing what others have already tried, by reading what others have already written. Indeed, in putting together this book, we were inspired by the amount of excellent analysis that already exists.

Just as Bush and his counterparts have been bold in their proposals, we must be innovative in our counter-proposals and our methods of organizing around them. Some of the international institutions and norms necessary to advance and enforce basic rights already exist. But we must create new ones that better fit the age of globalization. In an era when governments are crippled by fiscal crises and have bought into corporate agendas, we must forge new roles for civil society, nationally and internationally. Corporations have built international alliances based on hierarchy and profit maximization; we must build alternative alliances based on dialogue and respect for our differences. The free trade debate challenges us to work and think in ways which are new to all of us. Let us take up that hemispheric challenge.

John Cavanagh, a fellow at the Institute for Policy Studies, is co-author of Trade's Hidden Costs: Worker Rights in a Changing World Economy *(Washington, DC: ILRERF, 1988) and other books on the world economy. He is currently writing a book on the age of globalization with Richard Barnet.*

Footnotes

1. Quoted in, "Latin countries should be like pretty girls," *Philippine Daily Globe,* June 28, 1991.
2. Prepared Statement to the US House Foreign Affairs Subcommittee on Western Hemispheric Affairs, March 5, 1991.
3. Quoted in Keith Bradsher, "Trade Pact Soon Called Unlikely," *New York Times,* August 5, 1991.
4. See a series of memoranda prepared by Karen Hansen-Kuhn and Steve Hellinger of the Development GAP, Washington, DC, on the European Social Fund and European Regional Development Fund, July 1991.

1. Free Trade in Context

The division of labor among nations is that some specialize in winning and others in losing. Our part of the world, known today as Latin America, was precocious: it has specialized in losing ever since those remote times when Renaissance Europeans ventured across the ocean and buried their teeth in the throats of the Indian civilizations. Centuries passed, and Latin America perfected its role. We are no longer in the era of marvels when fact surpassed fable and imagination was shamed by the trophies of conquest – the lodes of gold, the mountains of silver. But our region still works as a menial. It continues to exist at the service of others' needs, as a source and reserve of oil and iron, of copper and meat, of fruit and coffee, the raw materials and foods destined for rich countries which profit more from consuming them than Latin America does from producing them. The taxes collected by the buyers are much higher than the prices received by the sellers; and after all, as Alliance for Progress coordinator Covey T. Oliver said in July 1968, to speak of fair prices is a 'medieval' concept, for we are in the era of free trade.

Eduardo Galeano
Open Veins of Latin America

Introduction

John Gershman
The proposal for a North American Free Trade Agreement (NAFTA) represents the latest in a series of initiatives by the United States to restructure the world economy. The issues relating to the NAFTA are also central to debates about the world economy more broadly. This section places debates about the NAFTA in the context of dramatic changes in the world economy and the global dimension of free trade.

The Global Assembly Line
The rise of the transnational corporation in the world economy has globalized production, leading to 'world cars' and global supermarkets. John Cavanagh and associates discuss how this transformation has altered patterns of trade and investment throughout the world.

The transnational corporation poses a central challenge to the conventional wisdom of development. That wisdom claims that governments and communities must provide 'good business climates' for corporate investment, laying the foundation for the increased standards of living which will ensue. John Gaventa's case study of the Jim Robbins Seat Belt Company illustrates how competition to provide the best business climate sets communities against each other, with drastic impacts on workers and communities. Rather than striving to create communities which provide the cleanest environment and meet the basic needs of all, the competition becomes one of providing the lowest wages, the largest tax breaks, and the least regulation. In a world of global production and transnational corporations, Gaventa's case study illustrates that debates about trade and investment are not simply local or national issues, but international in scope.

The Global Agenda
The General Agreement on Tariffs and Trade (GATT) has served as the organizing framework for global trade negotiations since the end of World War II. David Morris discusses the impact of economic policies of free trade and 'export at all costs' on the ecological and economic foundation of sustainable and viable communities.

The latest round of GATT negotiations began in 1986 in Punta del Este, Uruguay. This Uruguay Round of negotiations includes an unprecedented agenda, including foreign investment, services, agriculture, and intellectual property rights. The inclusion of these issues poses major challenges to developing ecologically sustainable economies as well as insuring national sovereignty for countries of the South. Robert Schaeffer describes how GATT decisions could undermine national and local environmental legislation and accelerate environmental degradation.

The Uruguay Round promises to increase the power and freedom of movement of transnational corporations while dramatically limiting the ability of poor countries to regulate them. This wholesale assault on sovereignty is the subject of Martin Khor's discussion of the threat that the Uruguay Round poses to the ability of the Southern countries to harness foreign investment to serve development objectives.

Lessons from Canada

The Canada-US Free Trade Agreement is the foundation for the proposed NAFTA. The final section combines an assessment of the impact of nearly three years of free trade on the Canadian economy and the US and Canadian environment.

The Mulroney Administration promised a future of prosperity with the negotiation of a Canada-US FTA. Bruce Campbell discusses how this prosperity remains an unfulfilled promise as he chronicles the destructive impact of the FTA on Canadian workers.

Steven Shrybman challenges claims that the FTA had no impact on the environment or environmental policy. He explains how the Canada-US FTA 'sold the environment short' by creating a framework wherein environmental regulations are and will continue to be undermined by labelling them as non-tariff barriers to trade.

Maude Barlow and George Watts conclude with their compelling testimony of the negative impact of the FTA on Canadians. Barlow's indictment of the Canada-US FTA as a 'corporate bill of rights' eloquently captures the character of the Canada-US FTA, while George Watts articulates an indigenous perspective on the NAFTA, concluding with a call to think about the children whose lives will be shaped by continental free trade.

John Gershman is a research associate at the Institute for Food and Development Policy.

The Global Assembly Line

The Transnational Corporation

John Cavanagh, Lance Compa, Allan Ebert, Bill Goold, Kathy Selvaggio, and Tim Shorrock

The transnational corporation is the first modern human institution with the money and technology to plan on a global scale. To maximize profits, it breaks production processes into components and locates each part where it will contribute most to the bottom line.

In the electronics industry, for example, circuits are printed on silicon wafers and tested in California; the wafers are then shipped to East Asia where they are cut into tiny chips and bonded to circuit boards. The final assembly for video games, computers, military equipment, and other products is usually performed back in the US.

A major inducement for corporate investment overseas, particularly in the Third World, is the free trade zone. Over 50 developing countries have set up these zones – sometimes called 'export processing zones' – at the urging of international bankers and foreign transnational corporations.

In recent years, offshore assembly has spread far beyond light manufacturing. For example, American automobile manufacturers now make engine and transmission parts in locations as diverse as Brazil, Mexico, South Korea, and Japan, bringing the finished components back to US assembly lines. The auto companies also import small cars as well as major components of larger cars from overseas.

Examples abound in other industries. Three thousand steelworkers in a Geneva, Utah plant were displaced by a Korea-based joint venture between the Korean government-owned Pohang Iron and Steel Co. and USX Corp. (formerly US Steel). Copper from Chile undercuts the price of copper mined by US workers. Kitchen appliances from Taiwan cause plant shutdowns and layoffs in the US. Even 'growth' industries like telecommunications have become part of the global assembly line. A recent US Congressional study concluded that offshore investments by US firms in the Pacific Rim and Mexico were a "major reason" for the growing trade deficit in high technology goods – estimated at $2 billion in 1986.[1]

The Hollow Corporation

During the 1980s, high interest rates in the US and the continuing availability of exploited labor in the Third World has transformed many leading manufacturers into supermarkets for goods produced overseas. This trend was recently analyzed by *Business Week* magazine, which dubbed the new version of American business 'The Hollow Corporation':

> The result is the evolution of a new kind of company; manufacturers that do little or no manufacturing and are increasingly becoming service-oriented. They may perform a host of profit-making functions – from design to distribution – but lack their own production base. In contrast to traditional manufacturers, they are hollow corporations.[2]

According to this analysis, companies are 'hollowing out' in several ways. Some shift technology and capital investment abroad to take advantage of cheap foreign labor: it has been estimated that 20 percent of all new jobs created by American capital investment are overseas. Some companies have entered into joint ventures, as USX did with Pohang, buying the raw materials or components abroad and preparing them for sale here. Others – such as Caterpillar Tractor Co. and General Electric – are contracting entire products out to foreign manufacturers and selling them here under their own brand names.

But whether their products are made in Pennsylvania or Korea, the power of transnational corporations rests in large measure in their ability to generate exports, an ability that is strengthened by economic policies throughout the world favoring production for the world market over production for domestic use. In this sense, the development of the 'Hollow Corporation' is the reverse side of the export-oriented economic plans adopted in South Korea, Taiwan, and other countries, including the US.

For example, tax and other incentives offered by governments often encourage exports and investments abroad rather than the development of domestic markets. US tariff laws encourage US corporations to locate facilities abroad to process raw materials for export back to the US. In December 1986, organized labor and a number of members of Congress protested when the US Department of Commerce planned to sponsor a three-day trade show in Mexico City designed to promote new US investments in maquiladoras on the Mexican side of the border. Called 'Expo Maquila 1986,' the show attracted hundreds of American businessmen.

"To use our tax money to fund and operate a program designed to lure jobs and capital out of the US is unconscionable," several Representatives wrote to Commerce Secretary Malcolm Baldrige. They urged that funds allocated to the trade show be "instead applied not toward diminishing opportunities for the American worker, but rather toward educating and training our own American workers so that our work force can better fill the needs here at home, and keep pace with our rapidly changing work environment."

With such encouragement of capital mobility, it is hardly surprising that an estimated 40 percent of world trade is composed of transactions between units of the same corporation. A 1985 study based on data from the Commerce Department showed that the amount of sales back to the US from affiliates of American corporations came to 28 percent of official import figures. That means that of every dollar of imports recorded in US accounts, 28 cents came from affiliates of American corporations.[3]

As American University professor and author Howard Wachtel points out, "the image that is usually conjured up of Japanese automobiles invading the West Coast and then the rest of the country through Long Beach, California, is only partially correct. [The US is] also being invaded ... by General Motors, by Ford, by Chrysler, and the same is true in every other industry."[4]

John Cavanagh, a fellow at the Institute for Policy Studies, co-directs IPS' World Economy Project with Richard J. Barnet. Lance Compa, a specialist on international labor rights, works for the Newspaper Guild. Allan Ebert is an immigration lawyer in Washington, DC. Bill Goold is chief of staff for Congressman Don Pease (D-Ohio). Kathy Selvaggio is a development specialist in Washington, DC. Tim Shorrock writes on labor and trade issues. This is excerpted from Trade's Hidden Costs *(Washington, DC: International Labor Rights Education and Research Fund, 1988).*

Footnotes

1. *Washington Post*, October 21, 1986.
2. *Business Week*, March 3, 1986, p. 57.
3. Figures from the statement of Howard Wachtel at March 6, 1986, Capitol Hill conference on 'Labor Rights and the Trade Debate.' See p. 54 of written transcript.
4. *Ibid.*

Capital Flight and Workers

John Gaventa

In recent years the US economy has lost hundreds of thousands of jobs in manufacturing. According to a study by the Office of Technology Assessment, in the years between 1979 and 1985, 11.5 million workers lost their jobs as companies decided to shut down or relocate manufacturing plants, increase productivity, or shrink output. These plant closings and layoffs have prompted warnings of the 'deindustrialization of America,' and have caused major disruptions in workers' lives.[1]

Until recently, the South was often thought to be exempt from these trends. In fact, for decades deindustrialization of the Frost Belt North meant the growth of the Sun Belt South. The South was on the receiving end of capital mobility, as runaway shops from the North came south in search of a 'favorable business climate' – meaning low-wage labor, cheap resources, and community subsidies. But by the early 1980s, the trend began changing, and the industries that had once moved to the South also began to close or relocate overseas. As Southern economic historian James Cobb writes, "Industries fleeing the South are purchasing one-way tickets to Taiwan and other exotic destinations just as readily as they used to depart Akron, Ohio for Opelika, Alabama."[2]

Why are plants leaving, and where are they going? Do workers in the Sun Belt experience problems of dislocation similar to those of other regions? The following case study provides a classic story of the movement of capital from the North, to the South, to the Third World, in constant search of cheaper labor and a more favorable business climate.

The Move to the Appalachian South

The Jim Robbins Seat Belt Company was originally based in Michigan and first considered Knoxville, Tennessee, as a plant site in the early 1960s. The mood of the time encouraged industrial growth and expansion. Demand for seat belts was also growing, and the company moved rapidly to meet it.

Early one morning in November 1965, Robbins' chief executive officer telephoned the industrial development executive of the Knoxville Chamber of Commerce about possible sites for the new plant. That same afternoon, corporate officials arrived in Knoxville in an executive jet, piloted by the company owner, Jim Robbins. A lease on an abandoned Du Pont facility was signed. The following Monday the company began hiring 50 workers. Within two weeks employment was up to 100, with two shifts daily producing 50,000 belts a week – all under contract with Ford and General Motors.

By 1967 local employment had risen to 1,200 people, and production to 60,000 assembled seat belts a day – enough to meet 60 percent of Ford's requirements and a large percentage of GM's. Local papers heralded the operation as the largest seat-belt manufacturing company in the world, producing more than 19 million belts a year.

The company heads cited Knoxville's favorable business atmosphere and the attitude of the workers as playing a big part in their decision to locate in the city. In 1967, the company president, Bill Johnson, praised Knoxville's "progressive local government," which was "interested in the requirements of industrial development." The city government had helped the company acquire land, cut through red tape for installation of utilities, and, in general, displayed a "cooperative spirit." "The workforce has a progressive attitude and a desire to work which is essential for industrial growth," Johnson said. "They're good workers and they're intelligent too. Your labor force here trains very quickly." Moreover, he stated bluntly, "The future of our expansion in Knoxville depends on the business atmosphere."[3]

The business atmosphere was also affected, of course, by wage differentials between Michigan and Tennessee. In 1972, according to the US Census of Manufacturers, the average wage for production workers in the industry in Knoxville was $2.58 an hour, about half the $5.04 an hour that similar workers received in the Detroit area.

By 1979, the company employed almost 3,000 workers and ranked, with two other textile firms, Levi Strauss and Standard Knitting Mills, among the city's largest industrial employers.[4]

The Bubble Bursts: From Tennessee to Alabama

The atmosphere of industrial growth began to change very quickly in the 1980s. In an eight-month period during late 1979 and early 1980, the company laid off 1,500 employees. This was followed by a further series of layoffs, bringing employment down by between 300 and 400 workers by 1983.

At first, in 1981, company officials publicly attributed the layoffs to the deepening effects of the recession on the automotive industry. By 1983, as the country climbed out of the recession, the company blamed the slump in new US car sales and increased imports.

However, at the same time that the company was saying it could not afford to reinvest in Knoxville, it was investing handsomely in a new facility in Greensville, Alabama, a rural, nonunion area anxious to acquire new industry. Between 1980 and 1985 the company carried out three expansions there and increased its Alabama work force threefold, from 300 in 1980 to 960 in 1985.

In Alabama, the company echoed the story that Knoxville officials had heard 15 years before. The company needed room to expand. Greensville offered a "large and motivated workforce, most easily trainable and many already seasoned in industrial sewing, thanks to the area's history of textile and carpet production." Moreover, the strong work ethic of the local labor force was complemented by the "upbeat, co-operative, ready-to-serve attitude of local officials and business leaders."[5]

As Knoxville had 15 years earlier, Greensville responded quickly. The mayor's office, the Industrial Development Board, and local banks provided revenue-bond financing for the purchase of the first building in 1980, and another in 1982. The Alabama Development Office helped the company by providing a training program in sewing and assembly, and by handling all employee recruiting and prescreening.[6]

As in the move to Tennessee, differences in wages were also a factor. Butler County, where Greensville is located, is more rural than Knoxville, with fewer unions and fewer industrial competitors. In 1982, wages for manufacturing workers in Butler County were approximately 60 percent of those for similar workers in Knoxville.[7]

Rather than reinvest in equipment and retraining in Knoxville, the company moved to a new area that offered cheaper, nonunion labor and favorable state subsidies. Moreover, as the company increased its facilities in Alabama, it used the threat of further layoffs and movement of capital to exact concessions from the Knoxville work force. By the 1980s, "the company increasingly used job blackmail against us, playing Knoxville workers off against the Alabama employees," said one local union official.

In 1983, the company offered to bring some of the jobs back to Knoxville, but only if workers there would reduce job classifications and accept pay cuts. Desperate for jobs, the union members accepted the offer, returning to work for wages lower than those rejected three years before. "We're hoping it will be a start of a major turnaround," the union official said at the time. "It's definitely a trend going in the right direction."[8]

The optimism did not last long. Not long after a few jobs returned to Knoxville from Alabama, they were transferred again – this time to new plants in Mexico. In August 1985, more than 200 workers were laid off, leaving employment at slightly above 200 in an area that only six years before had been declared the seat-belt capital of the world.

From the Mountains to the Maquiladoras

For its new seat-belt facility, the company chose the town of Aqua Prieta, one of the smaller and newer maquiladora border towns. Located in the state of Sonora, directly across the border from Douglas, Arizona, the town of Aqua Prieta is typical.[9] In recent years more than 20 manufacturing plants have located in the town, almost all of them sewing, electronics, automotive parts, or other labor-intensive operations from the US. With factory work abundant, the population has more than tripled in 10 years, from 18,000 in the mid-1970s to more than 60,000 people by the mid-1980s. The new seat-belt plant opened on January 1, 1986. According to sources in the plant, the company employs about 500 people and is growing. There, in repetitive, noisy, assembly-line work, the workers cut the webbing and assemble the seat-belts for shipment back to Greensville for US distribution. The wages are minuscule, compared to those in the US. Workers in this plant, as in others along the Mexican border, work 9 $1/2$-hour days for about $3.50 a day, or 37 cents an hour, one-sixteenth of the wages workers received for comparable work in Knoxville.

Although the wages seem low to the US visitor, the jobs are on the whole welcomed by local workers. Bumper stickers on cars parked near the plant claim in Spanish, 'I love Bendix.' (By then the seat-belt company was the Bendix division of a large conglomerate.) Local merchants are glad of the revenues. Even the local union, which is tied into the official national union, does little to question the arrangement. In short, the business climate is very, very favorable. As one US resident along the border told me, "If you think economic boosterism is big in your part of the world, you haven't seen anything until you come here."

It may be more intense, but this pro-business climate arises out of a very familiar development policy: recruit industry from the North. In Mexico, the maquiladora zone has emerged as the official solution to regional underdevelopment. But to large multinational businesses like the seat-belt company, it is simply one more area in the world economy that, desperate for development at any price, will provide cheaper labor and a more favorable business climate.

Multinationals: Mergers and Conglomeration

As the seat-belt company moved from the North to the urban South, then to the rural nonunion South, then to Mexico, it also was becoming integrated into a larger multinational corporate empire. When the company came to Knoxville in 1965, it was a private venture owned by Jim Robbins, a self-made Michigan millionaire, with holdings ranging from banana and cotton plantations in Venezuela to seat-belt and plastics factories in the Detroit area. A year later the firm was brought by the Allied Chemical Corporation, a vast chemical and manufacturing firm. In 1982, Allied took over the Bendix Corporation, and in 1983 the seat-belt operation became the Bendix Safety Restraint Division.

In 1985, Allied merged with the Signal Corporation to form Allied Signal, now one of the largest manufacturing holding firms in the world. As workers in Knoxville were being laid off as a result of the movement of their jobs to Mexico, top officials of Allied and Signal were receiving at least $50 million in cash, stock giveaways, options, and other benefits in what *The Wall Street Journal* marked as one of the largest windfalls for corporate executives in merger history.[10]

John Gaventa is an assistant professor of sociology at the University of Tennessee and director of the Highlander Research and Education Center. This is excerpted from his chapter in Communities in Economic Crisis: Appalachia and the South *edited by John Gaventa, Barbara Ellen Smith, and Alex Willingham (Philadelphia: Temple University Press, 1990).*

Footnotes

1. US Congress, Joint Economic Committee, *The Great American Job Machine: The Proliferation of Low-Wage Employment in the US Economy*, study prepared by Barry Bluestone and Bennett Harrison, December 1986. US Congress, Office of Technology Assessment, *Technology and Structural Unemployment: Reemploying Displaced Adults*, OTA-ITE 250 (Washington, DC, US Government printing Office, 1986), p. 5. For effects of layoffs, see Barry Bluestone and Bennett Harrison, *The Deindustrialization of America: Plant Closings, Community Abandonment and the Dismantling of Basic Industry* (New York: Basic Books, 1982), and Robert B. Reich, "The Hollow Corporation" *Business Week*, March 3, 1986.

2. James C. Cobb, "The Southern Business Climate: A Historical Perspective," *Forum for Applied Research and Public Policy* 1, no.2 (Summer 1986) p. 98.

3. *Knoxville News Sentinel*, November 29, 1967. Text of speech by Mr. Bill Johnson, "The Decision to Locate in Knoxville and Resulting Success," November 30, 1967.

4. In the summer of 1988, both Levi's and Standard announced they were closing down their Knoxville operations.

5. *Nation's Business*, May 1985, 40J.

6. Ibid.

7. Based on US Department of Commerce, Bureau of the Census, Census of Manufacturers, 1982. Data on wages of textile and apparel workers in Butler County were not available.

8. Quoted in *Knoxville News Sentinel*, November 23, 1983. Information about Knoxville worker concessions derived from interviews with local union officials and from a comparison of "Agreements between Allied Corporation … and Amalgated Clothing and Textile Workers Union," December 1, 1980, with agreements dated March 15, 1982, and December 1, 1985.

9. Observations about Aqua Prieta are based on personal visit and interviews, September 24-26, 1987.

10. *The Wall Street Journal*, August 12, 1985.

The Global Agenda

Free Trade: The Great Destroyer
David Morris

The planetary economy merges nations. Yoshitaka Sajima, vice president of Mitsui and Company (USA), asserts: "The US and Japan are not just trading with each other anymore – they've become part of each other." The US and Canadian governments have signed a free trade agreement to merge the two countries. One of the key provisions in the treaty is Canada's agreement to allow foreign ownership of its productive assets. Northern Mexico is all but integrated into the US economy through tremendous growth of the maquiladoras – factories that use US-made intermediary products and raw materials to manufacture or assemble final products for re-export into the US. By the turn of the century, the industrial heartland of North America may be on the other side of the Texan and New Mexican border. Meanwhile, in Europe, the Common Market has grown from six countries in the 1950s, to 10 in the 1970s, to 12 today, and barriers between these nations are rapidly being abolished. Pressure is now on the fiercely independent Scandinavian countries to join. Increasingly there are no Italian or French or German companies but only European super-corporations.

Export promotion is now widely accepted as the foundation for successful economic development – witness the success of the newly-industrializing countries like South Korea, Taiwan, and Singapore. Whether by a tiny country like Singapore or a huge country like the US, ever-growing exports are viewed as essential to the nation's economic health. In Minnesota, the former Department of Energy and Economic Development has become the Department of Trade and Economic Development. The energy division has moved to another agency. The change is revealing for two reasons. The energy program's main goal was to reduce Minnesota's reliance on imported energy, to promote self-reliance by tapping into local resources and encouraging higher efficiency. Today, the Department's principal goal is to make Minnesota more dependent on the rest of the world.

Destroying Communities

Free trade demands that we treat our neighbors no differently than we treat distant peoples with different customs, language, and culture. Planetism rearranges our loyalties and loosens our neighborly ties. As the *New York Times* puts it, "The new order eschews loyalty to workers, products, corporate structure, businesses, factories, communities, even the nation." Martin S. Davis, chairman of Gulf and Western, goes further. "All such allegiances are viewed as expendable under the new rules. You cannot be emotionally bound to any particular asset." We are now assets.

Jettisoning loyalties is not easy. But that is the price we pay to receive the material benefits of the 'global village.' Every community must achieve the lowest possible production cost even when that means companies breaking whatever remains of their social contract with communities. Stanley J. Mihelick, executive vice-president for production at Goodyear, is explicit: "Until we get real wage levels down much closer to those of the Brazils and Koreas, we cannot pass along productivity gains to wages and still be competitive." Wage rises, environmental protection, national health insurance, liability lawsuits, anything that raises the cost of production makes us less competitive and threatens our economy.

Never before have we so markedly and publicly expressed the need for the planetary economy to destroy local cultures. More and more human relationships have been transformed into commercial transactions. We have moved from diversified to specialized economies – separating the producer from the consumer, the farmer from the kitchen, the power plant from the appliance, the dump site from the dust bin, the banker from the borrower and depositor and, inevitably, the government from the citizenry. Development becomes a process by which we separate authority and responsibility, where those who make the decisions are not those affected by the decisions. Moreover, the planetary economy demands planetary institutions. Just as *Homo sapiens* is assumed to be nature's highest achievement, so the supranational corporation becomes our most highly evolved economic animal.

The Doctrine Falters

Yet at this very moment in history, when the doctrines of free trade and globalism are so dominant, we find more and more people raising doubts. Two hundred years ago, Benjamin Franklin warned: "The man who would trade independence for security deserves to wind up with neither." Willfully and consciously, we have made that trade.

The absurdities of globalism are becoming ever more evident. Consider the case of the toothpick and the chopstick. A few years ago, I was eating at a restaurant in Saint Paul, Minnesota. After lunch, I picked up a toothpick wrapped in plastic. On the plastic was the word 'Japan.' Now Japan has little wood and no oil. Yet in our global economy, it is deemed efficient to send little pieces of wood and some barrels of oil to Japan, wrap the one with the other and send them back to Minnesota. This toothpick may embody 50,000 miles of travel. Meanwhile, in 1987, a Minnesota factory began producing millions of disposable chopsticks a year for sale in Japan. In my mind's eye, I see two ships passing one another in the northern Pacific. One carries little pieces of Minnesota wood bound for Japan; the other carries little pieces of wood from Japan bound for Minnesota. Such is the logic of free trade.

Two centuries of trade has not evened up disparities in world living standards but exacerbated them. According to Swiss economist Paul Bairoch, per capita gross national product in 1750 was approximately the same in the developed countries as in the underdeveloped ones. In 1930, the ratio was about 4 to 1 in favor of the developed. Today it is 8 to 1.

Consider the plight of the Third World. Developing nations borrowed enormous sums of money to create the infrastructure to specialize in what they do best and to expand their export capacity. To repay the loans, these countries had to increase their exports even more to earn internationally acceptable currencies. One result has been a dramatic shift in their agricultural resources from producing food for internal consumption to producing food for export. Economists point to increased exports of wheat and soybeans from the developing world as evidence of their progress. But take the case of Brazil. Brazilian per capita production of basic foodstuffs (rice, black beans, manioc, and potatoes) fell 13 percent from 1977 to 1984. Per capita output of exportable foodstuffs (soybeans, oranges, cotton, peanuts and tobacco) jumped 15 percent. Today some 50 percent of Brazil's population suffers from malnutrition. Yet one leading Brazilian agronomist still calls export promotion, "a matter of national survival." In the global village, a nation survives by starving its people.

Even in the US, the most developed of all nations, free trade has not prevented living standards from declining over the last 15 years. Americans work almost half a day longer today for lower real wages than in 1970. Less leisure time means less time with the family and community. If the present trend continues, we may have less leisure time in the 1990s than we had in the 1970s. Clearly, it is time to re-examine the doctrine of free trade and its corollary, the planetary economy.

David Morris is co-director of the Washington, DC-based Institute for Local Self-Reliance. This is excerpted from his article of the same name that originally appeared in The Ecologist *Vol. 20, No.5 (September/October 1990).*

Trading Away the Planet

Robert Schaeffer

Since 1948 international trade has been governed in part by the General Agreement on Tariffs and Trade (GATT). GATT is a rule book that establishes how companies in different countries should buy and sell their products. About once every five years, the world's trade ministers meet, usually at the urging of the US, to renegotiate the rules of the agreement. For the most part, these reforms have been restricted to encouraging nations to stop placing taxes on foreign goods.

Five years ago, the world's trade ministers met at a posh seaside resort to begin the Uruguay Round of negotiations. This time, the US is pushing for a bigger prize. They want the rule book to be rewritten and expanded to permit international corporations to set up shop in any corner of the world with as little government interference as possible. This means free access to natural resources with a minimum of social and environmental 'strings' attached – few regulations, emissions standards or other hedges against pollution, habitat loss, or exploitation of labor. Any nation that decides to impose limits on the rights of foreign companies, for environmental or social reasons, can be retaliated against for creating a 'restraint on trade.'

The Bush administration will present the new GATT as a more perfect realization of 'free trade.' Through arrangements like the recent trade agreement between Canada and the US, and the 'borderless Europe' of 1992, national governments are organizing the global economy around this definition of free trade.

Many scholars, environmentalists, labor, and human rights activists and Third World leaders are strongly opposed to the notion of free trade as defined by corporate interests and their allies in the US government. If the US gets its way in the Uruguay Round, they contend that much of the authority to protect the environment, food, labor, and small businesses will be taken from communities, states, and nations and put in the hands of government-appointed trade ministers, multinational corporations, and obscure international agencies.

In 1981, in response to a growing garbage crisis, Denmark passed a law requiring that beer and soft drinks be sold only in returnable bottles. In 1987, the European Commission took Denmark to the European Court of

Justice, arguing that the law was an unfair restraint on free trade because it imposed, in the words of *The Economist*, a "disproportionate level of environmental protection." The court backed Denmark, but only on returnable bottles. A plan to demand refillable bottles from industry was struck down as a restraint on trade.

Canada's western forests are also victims of free trade. After being pushed by the Bush administration, British Columbia ended a government-funded, tree-planting program. Planting trees, the US argued, was an "unfair subsidy" to Canada's timber industry. This is how free trade can destroy the environment.

Health Standards

In recent years, California voters approved the anti-toxic Proposition 65, and state legislators have passed air-quality and waste-disposal regulations that are more stringent than federal law.

US negotiators are proposing to 'harmonize' standards governing food safety to eliminate what they call 'non-tariff' barriers to trade, such as food-labeling or recycling requirements. Instead of allowing local, state or national governments to set standards, US negotiators would make international standard-setting bodies, such as the UN's *Codex Alimentarius* Commission, responsible for creating uniform global food standards.

Because this tiny agency based in Rome sets extremely low standards for some commodities, the proposal to make Codex responsible for food safety would degrade protection for consumers and the environment. Current Codex standards, for example, would allow the import of bananas containing up to 50 times the amount of DDT permitted by the US Food and Drug Administration. It would allow a 10-fold increase of DDT residues in imported carrots and potatoes, a 20-fold increase in strawberries and grapes, and a 33-fold increase in pineapple, broccoli, and lettuce. Under GATT rules, if California, for example, attempted to set higher standards or restrict the import of food contaminated with pesticides now banned in the US, foreign governments could sue the US for establishing nontariff barriers to trade.

Natural Resources

US negotiators are eager to prevent countries from restricting food exports for any reason, even when they are facing food shortages at home. In addition, they want to eliminate export restrictions on natural resources, such as the raw log export bans adopted by Asian and Pacific nations to slow the destruction of the rainforests. GATT rules could make it extremely difficult for countries anywhere to develop their raw materials and natural resources on a sustainable basis. Proposed GATT rules could also prevent countries from restricting the import of goods, such as hazardous wastes, simply because they apply higher environmental standards than other countries.

Subsidies

US negotiators want to eliminate agricultural subsidies. US family farmers annually receive about $40 billion in aid from the federal government, most of it to support commodity prices, but some of it to promote soil and water conservation. This includes land set-aside programs designed to allow the soil to recover its natural fertility. All of this would go out the window if price supports were withdrawn and support for conservation-related farm activities were treated as 'trade-distorting subsidies.'

By changing GATT to prohibit government-funded agricultural programs, more land would be put to the plow. Commodity prices would fall, family farmers would be ruined, and land would be consolidated in the hands of corporate farmers. Under these conditions, groundwater contamination and soil loss would become even more serious. The conscientious family farmer may replenish or keep soil loss at a minimum, but the corporate farmer can lose up to 35-40 tons annually.

Technology

US and European negotiators want patents, trademarks, and other 'intellectual property rights' to be recognized internationally. While the reforms are advertised as an effort to stop bootlegging of US and European products such as watches, luggage, and audio recordings, the implications are considerably more far-reaching. For example, as corporate-controlled biotechnology advances, a poor Mexican farmer might find him/herself unable to afford seeds for drought-resistant tomatoes because the patent on the seeds is held by a US-based chemical corporation. This, despite the fact that the genetic material that established the plant's resistance to drought could well have originated in Mexico.

The US is asking nations around the world to surrender the authority to protect their environment, their workers, and their small businesses in pursuit of the notion of 'free trade.' The unquestioned assumption of this demand is that the unfettered access of major corporations to every corner of the world will produce a host of mutual benefits.

Contemporary free traders argue that GATT is responsible for the 10-fold increase in the volume of world trade since 1950. This may or may not be true (some economists argue that the increase in international trade is more the effect than the cause of the general increase in global wealth). But it is also beside the point. Increased trade has not made poor nations rich.

According to Giovanni Arrighi, an Italian economist who measured the gross national product per capita of countries around the world from 1938 to 1979, the global distribution of wealth has been rigidly stable, despite the expansion of trade. Arrighi's research found that the small number of rich countries stayed rich, the large number of impoverished countries remained poor by comparison, and a small group of intermediate-strata countries stayed where they were.

To put it simply, Guatemala was poor, and, despite free trade, it still is. When tariffs were averaging 40 percent in the 1940s, the US was extremely rich. Today they average four percent, but the gulf between the world's poor countries and the US remains as wide as it was in 1940. The only upwardly mobile countries during this period were Japan, South Korea, and Taiwan. But their success, Arrighi says, had more to do with internal economic policies and a special relationship with the US than with the effects of free trade.

Nor has free trade made the distribution of wealth within countries more equitable. The richest 20 percent of the population in Mexico earns 18 times the wealth of the poorest 20 percent; in Brazil, 28 times as much. Opening up Third World nations to unregulated foreign investment and services, as the new GATT would do, could just make things worse.

It is also questionable whether the consumers in rich countries benefit from any new freedoms granted multinational corporations. Concentrating power over markets in the hands of a few leads just as often to price-gouging monopolization as it does to trickle-down savings. In the 1980s, cocoa prices plummeted along with those of other basic Third World commodities, further impoverishing less-developed nations. But the price of a chocolate bar did not. The only thing that changed was the profit margin of the three companies that control the world cocoa market: Hershey's, Mars, and Nestle.

For the sake of simplicity, any analysis of any major international development should ask the question, 'Who will benefit?' In the case of the proposals to reform GATT, it is clear that the main beneficiaries will be a collection of international corporations that have no national loyalties. At risk are the global environment and the rights of people in California, Denmark, or Mexico to set policies protecting their health and their natural wealth.

Consumer advocate Ralph Nader accuses GATT "of imposing a mega-corporate view of the world. It is designed to circumvent democratic institutions and override local and state government efforts to protect consumers and the environment." As the twentieth century closes, the power that corporations wield over the workings of the planet is growing. At the same time, the power of people to assert their right to decide how to husband their natural resources and control their economic future is also on the rise.

The fight over GATT is really a fight over who will write the rules of international commerce – the corporations on behalf of their profits, or the people on behalf of the environment and the needs of the individual and the community. Speaking on behalf of a coalition of environmental groups, Lynn Greenwalt of the National Wildlife Federation said, "We have come together to note, and perhaps to prevent, the passing of an era – an era when local communities had a say in how their natural resources were used, and when state and federal governments could take steps to stop the destruction of our environment. These basic rights may be sacrificed by US negotiators in the name of free trade."

Robert Schaeffer is an assistant professor of sociology at San Jose State University. This is excerpted from his article in Greenpeace Magazine *(September/October 1990).*

Uruguay Round Threatens Third World Sovereignty

Martin Khor

Trade representatives of industrialized countries have been attempting a little-known but extremely dangerous assault on the economic sovereignty of Third World countries through the Uruguay Round talks under the auspices of the General Agreement on Tariffs and Trade (GATT).

The industrialized countries are attempting to extend and tighten their control of the world economy, in general, as well as over the national economies of Third World countries. They are seeking, in many areas of negotiations, to downgrade or remove entirely the 'development principle' which hitherto had been accepted within GATT rules.

According to the development principle, developing countries can be given exemptions or privileges from certain GATT obligations. This exemption is in recognition of the handicap they face as a result of lower economic development compared to the industrial countries, and in appreciation of the special needs they have in building up their long-term development capacity. In other words, the 'free trade' promoted by GATT was to be tempered with the 'development principle.'

In the current Uruguay Round negotiations, this principle has been eroded and ignored by the major industrial countries, which want Third World countries to be treated no differently than themselves. The industrial countries have also shown less interest in giving concessions in areas of Third World interest, such as improving access for Third World exports to markets in industrial countries.

Instead the real focus of the industrial countries' Uruguay Round agenda is to radically restructure GATT itself and immensely enlarge its powers so that it can become a 'world economic policeman' which enforces new rules that maximize the unimpeded operations of transnational corporations. Existing restrictions or obligations imposed by Third World governments on foreign companies are being portrayed as going against 'free trade.'

The transnational corporations want to remove barriers to their unimpeded activity so that they can penetrate Third World economies more effectively. An effective and well-organized lobby, they have enlisted their governments to make use of the Uruguay Round to extend free trade from merely manufactured goods to also embrace trade in agricultural products as well as the 'new themes' of services, investments, and intellectual property rights.

The Role of TNCs

In May 1990, leading US companies and business organizations announced the formation of a high-powered 'Multilateral Trade Negotiations (MTN) Coalition.' Chaired by the former US Trade Representative William Brock, now in private business, the group includes American Express, General Motors, IBM, General Electric, Cargill, Citicorp, Proctor & Gamble, as well as the US Council for International Business, American Business Conference, the National Association of Manufacturers, Coalition of Service Industries, International Investment Alliance, and the Intellectual Property Committee.

At the July 1990 Houston Summit of the Group of Seven (G-7), the MTN Coalition organized a high-powered press conference, where Brock said he found it "incredible" that the G-7 countries were unable to negotiate seriously, especially on agriculture, while the stakes in the Uruguay Round were so high. He said that while the Summit's focus was on farm reforms, "agriculture is not the issue ... Rather it is the linchpin to agreement on *issues of greater magnitude, issues that really matter*, like intellectual property protection, services, investments, and subsidies."

This clearly indicates that for the business sector, these new themes are the real agenda in the Uruguay Round. The President of the American Business Conference, Barry Rogstad, said US businessmen saw a strengthened GATT as the "single best way to create an environment to expand their international success."

Threatening Third World Sovereignty

If these new areas are incorporated into the GATT framework in the way proposed by the industrialized countries, then Third World countries will have to 'liberalize' or open up their national economies. This will allow transnational corporations to have sweeping rights not only to export to the

Third World, but to invest and set up operations in Third World countries, and to be treated like locally-owned companies, with hardly any state controls over them.

But the transnational corporations and the industrial countries want to have their cake and eat it too. They also propose that the GATT become the enforcer of new regimes on intellectual property rights. These would oblige Third World countries to have national laws granting patent rights and protection to transnational corporations for their products and technologies. This will severely hamper Third World companies or agencies from developing their own technological capacity and would grant monopoly power over technology to transnational corporations.

In fact, this goes against the principle of 'free trade' which the industrial countries are using as an argument to pry open the Third World. This contradiction exposes the double standards that underlie the industrial countries' self-interest in pushing for the adoption of 'new themes' or new powers to GATT. They use liberalism or free trade as an intellectual weapon to push for the liberalization of services and investment flows to the Third World; but they simultaneously want to restrict the free flow of technological capacity to the Third World by imposing patent obligations and intellectual property rights regimes onto the Third World.

The result is ever-expanding monopoly powers over larger geographical areas and in more economic sectors, controlled by fewer mega-companies. Facilitating this increasing concentration of capital and market power is what is the objective of the Uruguay Round. The flip side of this coin is the increasing erosion of Third World countries' control over their national economies to foreign enterprises and their increasing marginalization in the world economy.

Martin Khor is director of the Third World Network in Penang, Malaysia. This was excerpted from his article of the same name that appeared in Third World Network Features.

Lessons from Canada

The FTA: A Corporate Bill of Rights

Maude Barlow

Free trade removed the tools that Canadians had to set our own economic agenda. It removed the economic decision-making power in our country from the democratic process and turned it over to the private sector. And it's not even mostly the Canadian private sector.

Sometimes other countries tend to lump Canada and the US together. But we are a very different people. We have a different history, different culture, and different political values. For example, we have a very harsh geography. And it has forced us to share with one another for survival. Our most enduring legacy is the love of the land – harsh and unrelenting as it can be. Survival, not dominance, is central to our definition of self.

Our strong historical wish to live and resist the commercial links of the North-South pull led to the creation of national institutions to serve the people. A broadcasting system. A railway. An airline. National universal programs that distribute resources more equitably.

These were developed to link us – from fishing villages in the Newfoundland, across the prairies, and up to our North. And these are part of our character and history that we are losing. In its place is a new corporate-directed regime. We daily grow to resemble America's society: weakest to the wall, survival of the fittest, winner on top. This is what we mean by losing our sovereignty.

The US-Canada Free Trade Agreement is a corporate bill of rights, and also a blueprint for other deals to follow. The Royal Bank, one of our major banks, made this statement: "free trade breeds more free trade, putting pressure for other countries to come into line."

The transnational conglomerates are co-opting the world's nations. And in each country they have to find corporate and government sponsors to deliver the country and its people to them.

In Canada our corporate elite and our government became willing participants. So for our country a loss of sovereignty literally means a loss of democratic will of our people to establish the conditions under which these transnationals operate in our country.

The answers for us lie in reclaiming our democratic processes: within our communities, within our own country, and with the peoples of the world, to establish a new world trading order based on the great challenges of our day – common security, ecological stewardship, and international human rights.

Maude Barlow is the Chair of the Council of Canadians. This was excerpted from the Pro-Canada Dossier #29 *(January/February 1991).*

Beggar Thy Neighbor

Bruce Campbell

It became official in February 1991. The US-Mexico free trade negotiations will include Canada. Officials have indicated that the Canada-US Free Trade Agreement signed in 1988 will form the core of NAFTA, a reality which makes the Canadian perspective and experience instructive.

Several weeks after the Canada-US Free Trade Agreement (FTA) was signed, US Trade Representative Clayton Yeutter told a *Toronto Star* reporter, "The Canadians don't understand what they have signed. In 20 years they will be sucked into the US economy." Free trade critics understood very well. Author Margaret Atwood, testifying before a parliamentary committee, offered the following metaphor: "Our national animal is the beaver, noted for its industriousness and cooperative spirit. In medieval bestiaries it is also noted for its habit, when frightened, of biting off its own testicles and offering them to its pursuer." Was the FTA an act of national castration?

Historically, government has played an active role in the Canadian economy and society. Government has sought to manage the nation's rich natural resource base to ensure resource security, promote greater domestic processing or value added, and to provide comparative advantages to certain industries. Government has also used access to the national market as a development tool, for example, through tariffs or, as in the auto industry, through domestic content requirements.

Given the extraordinarily high level of foreign ownership (mainly US) of the manufacturing sector (50 percent) and key resource sectors (petroleum-75 percent), Canadian governments have regulated foreign-controlled companies with a view to ensuring their conduct confers 'net benefit to Canada.' Such benefit, we have learned, cannot be expected automatically.

The state has also been a vehicle for realizing Canadian values of community and social justice. There is national universal health care and established standards for collective bargaining, pay equity, health and safety, pesticide use, etc., which constitute the social and ethical 'rules' governing how companies do business in Canada. These standards have, for example, allowed unions to grow to 37 percent of the work force, helping to maintain relatively equitable patterns of income distribution. The record of Canadian government development policies contains both successes and failures. However, the power shift represented by the FTA – directly through specific provisions and indirectly through the inexorable pressure to harmonize the rules of competition downward to the lowest common denominator – has greatly reduced the 'policy space' available to governments to pursue national development and maintain social standards.

The Rise of Corporate Canada

Brian Mulroney came to power in 1984 with strong backing from corporate Canada. Free trade with the US was central to his neoconservative vision of the country's future. The conservative government had three main objectives in seeking a free trade deal: to secure and enhance access to the US market; to secure 'citizenship rights' for a small group of Canadian corporations which had been expanding and investing heavily in the US; and to use a trade deal as a lever to circumscribe and ratchet down the capacity of the government to meddle in the economy.

These goals were generally consistent with Washington's aims to secure rights for its own formidable corporate presence, as well as access to Canadian resources. The US also saw the FTA as a precedent, a wedge with teeth, to further its agenda in the GATT.

The November 1988 election was fought almost entirely on free trade. Mulroney promised that the FTA would bring jobs and prosperity for all Canadians in all regions. He denied jobs would be lost, yet he promised "massive adjustment programs." He claimed the FTA would strengthen government's capacity to maintain and improve social programs. But at the same time he sold it as a strictly commercial agreement which had nothing to do with social programs.

In fact, the agreement went far beyond the textbook definition of free trade. It was a sweeping economic integration pact covering labor mobility, capital mobility, resource management, services, and standards – as ambitious as Europe 1992.

Both major opposition parties, the Liberals and the New Democrats, opposed the deal, yet they failed to join forces. Grassroots resistance galvanized in the Pro-Canada Network, a broad coalition of farm and labor groups, women's groups, nationalists, environmentalists, church and social activists, and most of the cultural community.

The split within the opposition proved decisive. The FTA went into effect on January 1, 1989, and Brian Mulroney, who four years earlier had announced to the New York Economic Club that Canada was "open for business," returned to New York to receive an award as the Americas Society's 'Man of the Year.'

The Effects of Free Trade

The FTA was supposed to encourage restructuring on the basis of comparative advantage. Firms would become more efficient; output and income would increase. Workers would move from lower value-added jobs to higher ones. These expectations were based on four related assumptions, all at odds with reality: that Canada would enjoy secure access to the US market; that full employment in both economies already existed; that capital is relatively immobile beyond national borders; and that trade takes place between independent firms on an arm's length basis.

In the first place, the FTA did not secure access to the US market. Major barriers remained in such areas as steel (informal quotas), lumber (a 15% export tax), clothing (limitations on products with third-country fabrics), and sugar-based products (quotas). Furthermore, Canada did not gain exemption from US trade laws. On the contrary, the FTA actually legitimized US law, whether or not it contravened GATT law (article 1902.1) and permitted the US to change its laws at will (article 1902.2).

The FTA provided for negotiations to reach a common regime on subsidies/countervail and predatory pricing/anti-dumping by 1996. Many believe that these negotiations will never be concluded, since the US Congress is loathe to surrender its power to regulate trade. Moreover, the US implementing legislation (section 409) provides new weapons for harassing Canadian exporters suspected of using unfair subsidies. In the last two years the number of trade actions against Canadian exporters has actually increased; clothing, auto parts, meat, potato, and lumber exporters have all reported increased border delays and reinspections.[1]

Of the 17 cases that have come before the bi-national dispute-resolution panels created by the FTA, Canada has claimed one victory. In fact, exasperated steel executives have begun to criticize in public the inadequacies of a dispute mechanism which allows this heavily subsidized US industry to keep out Canadian products.

Some US experts are warning that Canada will not be exempt from new protectionist legislation. Elliot Richardson told a meeting of the Canada-US Business Association that the FTA would not protect Canada from proposed legislation restricting foreign investment. Even though this violates the accord, as Richardson points out, the US implementing legislation states that US law shall override the FTA in the case of a conflict. Canadian law is subordinate to the FTA.

Secondly, the assumption of full employment does not hold. Unemployment has not fallen below seven percent since the 1982 recession. Two years of free trade have seen the overall rate of job creation drop dramatically. If the previous five-year average had continued, the economy should have created an additional 650,000 new jobs in 1989-90. Although it can not be attributed exclusively to the FTA, the actual figure was 50,000.[2]

The manufacturing work force, which had been more or less stable throughout the 1980s, shrank by 20 percent, or 435,000 jobs, between March 1989 and March 1991.[3] The Canadian Manufacturers Association predicts that half of these jobs will not return. The Ontario Ministry of Labour found that 65 percent of layoffs in the last two years were due to plant closures. This contrasts with the height of the 1982 recession when less than one quarter of layoffs resulted from closures.[4]

The service sector picked up only part of the slack in terms of job creation. And most of these were low-paying, low-skill jobs, often temporary or part-time. Officially, unemployment is now over 10 percent; when workers who have dropped out of the job market are accounted for, the rate is around 15 percent.[5]

Thirdly, the first year of free trade set off a record wave of national and foreign takeovers of Canadian corporations, worth $27.7 billion, 40 percent higher than the previous year's total which was itself a record.[6] Takeovers subsided in 1990, but experts are predicting a second wave as the economy emerges from the recession. Forty percent of these (by value) involved foreign-controlled companies.

Statistics Canada, a government agency, reported that during 1988-1989, 460 Canadian-controlled companies, including major high technology firms (with combined assets of $21 billion), were taken over by foreign, primarily US, owners. During the same period only 13 foreign-controlled companies, with assets of $2.6 billion, were taken over by Canadian-controlled companies. As a result, foreign control of the economy jumped a full percentage point, reversing a 14-year downward trend.[7]

More recently, Investment Canada reported that in the two years leading up to April 1990, there were a record 1,403 foreign corporate takeovers of Canadian-based companies. The combined value of these takeovers was $30.5 billion. More than 90 percent of foreign corporate activity in Canada is in the form of takeovers, not new investment.[8]

The promised corporate restructuring has been a one-sided affair. Record numbers of mergers, takeovers, closures, downsizing, and rationalizations have destroyed thousands of jobs; free trade has not delivered the same number of higher value-added jobs. Lastly, a large part of Canada's manufacturing sector is made up of US-owned branch plant subsidiaries, which produce exclusively for the Canadian market. The FTA made it easier for branch plants to move. Rather than convert to export platforms, they have in large numbers shifted production to the Southern US and Mexico. All they left behind in Canada were warehouses and sales offices.[9]

Medium-size Canadian firms, which before free trade had threatened to move south to get behind US barriers, were now supposed to stay in Canada. Instead, the last two years have seen an exodus of Canadian firms across the border.[10] The testimony of a Quebec furniture manufacturer before a parliamentary committee explains why: " ... lower interest rates, something around five or six percent [sic] compared to 13 to 14 percent in Canada ... In some states we were offered for every new job created up to $2,000 ... Social benefit rates are much lower than in Canada ... What's more we can hire people at $4.50 an hour ... A number of states also have right-to-work legislation."[11]

Another part of the answer is illustrated in the experience of CCL Industries, a company which manufactures cans and other packaging products. The US transnationals which it supplied have shifted their purchasing operations south. The company survived only by moving 70 percent of its assets outside Canada, the reverse of the situation before free trade.

Bruce Campbell is a research fellow at the Canadian Center for Policy Alternatives. This is excerpted from his article of the same name in NACLA's Report on the Americas, *Vol. 24, No. 4 (May 1991).*

Footnotes

1. Senate Foreign Affairs Committee (Canada), "Monitoring the Implementation of the Canada-US Free Trade Agreement," March 1990, November 1990.
2. Statistics Canada Labor Force Survey, cited in *Toronto Globe and Mail*, May 24, 1989.
3. Statistics Canada.
4. Ontario Ministry of Labour, "Permanent and Indefinite Layoffs in Ontario," December 1990, December 1989, December 1982.
5. Andrew Jackson, "The 'Real' Rate of Unemployment," Canadian Labour Congress, mimeo, January 1991.
6. Venture Economics, Ltd., "Mergers and Acquisitions in Canada," December 1989. This and all figures in this article are stated in the US dollar equivalent.
7. Statistics Canada, in *Toronto Globe and Mail*, May 24, 1990.
8. Ontario Premier's Council Report, "Competing in the New Global Economy," cited in John O'Grady, "Labour Market Policy and Industrial

Strategy After the Free Trade Agreement," paper presented to the Industrial Relations Research Association, Buffalo, May 3, 1990.
9. I compiled a list of 50 branch plants that moved south in 1989-1990. It is by no means comprehensive.
10. I compiled a list of 27 such firms which fled.
11. Senate Foreign Affairs Committee (Canada), Proceedings, March 6, 1990, p.19:13.

Selling the Environment Short

Steven Shrybman

On January 1, 1989, Canada and the United State implemented a free trade agreement which in the words of President Reagan, represented an "economic constitution for North America." Ignoring commitments to integrated economic and environmental decision-making, and notwithstanding its obvious and far-reaching implications, both governments entirely ignored the environmental implications of the new trade regime. The Canadian Minister for International Trade responded to a question about the trade deal's environmental impact by stating:

> The free trade agreement is a commercial accord between the world's two largest trading partners. It is not an environmental agreement. The environment was not, therefore, a subject for negotiations nor are environmental matters included in the text of the agreement.[1]

But the trade deal was explicitly about energy and agricultural policies, forest management practices, food safety, and even pesticide regulation – matters that could not more directly affect the environment.

Promoting Energy Development and Use

An entire chapter of the Canada-US FTA is devoted to deregulating energy development and trade. Under the terms of the FTA both countries forego the use of regulatory devices that could be used to control the development of energy resources for export markets.[2] In addition, subsidies for oil and gas exploration and development are given special status under the agreement and insulated from attack under the trade protection laws of either country.[3] Subsidies and other programs intended to encourage energy efficiency and conservation measures are accorded no such protection.

The first and already observable effect of the deal has been to prompt a new round of energy mega-projects intended to serve US markets. Since the trade deal was implemented, export licenses have been granted for two of the largest energy projects in Canadian history.

One of the projects will involve extensive natural gas development in the Mackenzie Delta, on the shore of the Beaufort Sea in the Canadian Arctic. This $10 billion project will involve the construction of a 1,200 mile long pipeline, one of the longest in the world, across arctic permafrost. It will have significant and adverse environmental effects for unique and fragile northern ecosystems. Production facilities would be spread over a large area of the Mackenzie Delta, which is a major fish spawning, rearing, and over-wintering area, as well as a migratory corridor.[4] This project will be the largest ever undertaken in the Canadian Arctic and is being promoted by the Canadian subsidiaries of Esso, Gulf, and Shell – companies that vigorously supported the FTA.

The export licenses for this natural gas that have been approved by the National Energy Board (NEB) will allow the companies to export approximately 87 percent of the natural gas reserves of the Mackenzie Delta. It is impossible to reconcile a proposal that seeks to export approximately 87 percent of Mackenzie Delta gas reserves with any notion of resource conservation. The companies concede that the only rationale for arctic gas development at this time is to serve export markets in the US.[5] The other energy project that is a direct consequence of the economic and resource policies entrenched by the FTA is the James Bay hydro-electric development in Northern Quebec. Described by proponents as 'The Project of the Century', the James Bay II development will, when completed, produce a staggering 26,000 megawatts of power. It will reshape a territory the size of France and will be one of the largest engineering projects ever undertaken.[6]

As is true for the Mackenzie Delta gas reserves, the James Bay II project is being developed to serve export markets in the US. Its proponent is the Province of Quebec, the only province to come out strongly in favor of the FTA. So determined is the province to proceed with the project, regardless of its consequences for the environment or indigenous people, that it has passed legislation to weaken the environmental assessment and public hearing requirements that would apply to the project.

Fueling the Fire

The impacts of these energy mega-projects in Canada will be profound and are apparent. Less obvious, but no less significant, are their impacts in the US:

- Guaranteed access to Canada's energy resources will prolong the inefficient use of non-renewable resources by forestalling the impacts of declining US energy reserves.

- By assuring that the environmental impacts associated with large-scale energy developments occur in Canada rather than in the US, one of the most important incentives for conservationist policies in the US is held at bay.
- Flooding the market with cheap natural gas and electricity will displace conservation and efficiency investments that might have otherwise become cost-effective.

Mining the Forests and the Fisheries

Since the implementation of the FTA there has been a virtual explosion of proposals to establish large-scale logging and pulp operations in Canada. Virtually all of the proponents of these projects are transnational corporations based in the US or abroad. The implications of these projects for the prospects of sustainable forest management practices in Canada are disastrous because Chapter 4 of the FTA effectively precludes Canada from controlling the rate at which logs or pulp leave Canada for the US.

The first trade dispute under the FTA involved a challenge by the US to regulations under Canada's Fisheries Act established to promote conservation of herring and salmon stocks in Canada's Pacific coast waters.[7] This particular conservation program required that all fish commercially caught in Canadian waters be landed in Canada for biological sampling, to deter false reporting, and for in-season management. After reporting in this manner, US commercial fisherfolk were free to export to the US.

In the first dispute to be released under the FTA, the dispute panel determined that the Canadian regulations were, "incompatible with the requirements of Article 407 of the FTA." As explained by Robert Morley, executive director of the Fisheries Council of British Columbia:

> What the panel decision actually does is strike down a legitimate resource conservation scheme and recommend substitution of an expensive, loophole-laden, unmanageable dual reporting system.[8]

Undermining Environmental Regulation

By characterizing environmental laws as non-tariff barriers to trade, opponents of environmental and workplace health and safety regulation have used the FTA as a potent new weapon with which to assail these important initiatives.

The Canadian government has recently relied upon the FTA to challenge the US Environmental Protection Agency (EPA) asbestos regulations. In July 1989, the EPA announced it was introducing regulations to phase out the production, import, and use of asbestos over seven years. The ban represented the culmination of over 10 years of struggle that involved several Congressional investigations, 45,000 pages of analyses, comments and testimony, and thousands of lives.[9] Mr. Reilly, the EPA administrator, estimated that the ban on this cancer-causing material could save 1,900 lives by the turn of the century.[10] The case is presently in court.

In a similar vein the US non-ferrous metals industry has used a provision of the US legislation implementing the FTA to challenge, as unfair trade practices, a variety of Canadian programs. These programs are intended to reduce emissions from, and improve workplace safety in, several Canadian lead, zinc, and copper smelters. The US Trade Representative has determined that there is "a reasonable likelihood" that this complaint is well-founded and investigated these Canadian pollution control programs.

Because of free trade in hazardous waste, at least one Canadian hazardous waste management company advertises the absence of stringent US liability requirements as an incentive to attract US business. When the US was considering strengthening hazardous waste export controls to require that other jurisdictions meet US standards before exports to that jurisdiction would be approved, the Canadian government became the principal lobby opposing the initiative.[11]

With two exceptions, the Canada-US FTA is silent on the subject of environmental standards. Those exceptions concern the technical standards used at the federal level and pesticide and food safety standards. In each case the provisions of the FTA are intended to promote harmonization of standards, testing procedures, and regulations. The question that arises is whether harmonization requirements will raise or lower standards to a new common denominator.

In Canada pesticides are licensed pursuant to the provisions of the Pest Control Products Act, which places emphasis squarely upon demonstrating the safety of the pesticide at issue. In contrast, US pesticide legislation requires a balancing of risks and benefits, an approach environmentalists have argued against for years. The differences between the two approaches are quite real. In the US there are 20 percent more active pesticide ingredients registered for use and over seven times as many pesticide products.

One pertinent example is the herbicide alachlor, a probable human carcinogen, which the US continues to license but is banned in Canada. According to Canadian Health and Welfare officials, the evidence of carcinogenicity was the most convincing they had ever seen for a pesticide. Yet the US found that the benefits outweighed the risks of alachlor and continues to register it. Not surprisingly, the manufacturer has argued that Canada's licensing criteria should also be founded upon a risk/benefit criteria.

Specific examples of adverse environmental impacts of the FTA are, of course, very helpful in revealing the relationships between the environment and trade. However, it is the structural and economic realities of free trade that will give rise to its most serious and adverse environmental impacts. To understand these cause and effect relationships it is important to recognize that many of the environmental issues we confront are the symptoms, and not the causes, of unsustainable economic and resource policies.

Steven Shrybman is currently on leave from the Canadian Environmental Law Association, serving as a senior policy advisor in the Cabinet Office of the Government of Ontario. This was excerpted from Selling the Environment Short: An Environmental Assessment of the First Two Years of Free Trade between Canada and the US *(Canadian Environmental Law Association, May 1991).*

Footnotes

1. The federal Minister for International Trade in response to a question on the House of Commons order paper during the fall of 1987; see Frank Tester, "Free Trading the Environment" in *The Free Trade Deal* (Toronto: Lorimer & Company, 1988).

2. Article 904 of the Canada-US Free Trade Agreement explicitly prevents either government from restricting the export of energy resources, for any other than "national security" reasons, unless supplies are rationed, to the same extent, domestically. The important right under the GATT rules to use export taxes as a mechanism for resource management and conservation, is abolished by the agreement. For example, compare with Article XX of GATT. Bill C-130, that implemented the Agreement in Canada, abolishes a central tenet of Canadian energy policy and compels the NEB to issue an export license even in the face of Canadian shortages. While the NEB may attach terms and conditions to its approval, it cannot refuse a license for environmental reasons.

3. Article 906 provides: "Both parties have agreed to allow existing or future incentives for oil and gas exploration, development, and related activities in order to maintain the reserve base for future energy resources." The only other category of government subsidy that is accorded this special status is defense spending.

4. Marbek Resource Consultants, *A Preliminary Assessment of the Applicants' Submissions to the Environmental Screening of Gas Export Licenses Issued under GH-10-88*, September 1990.

5. NEB reasons for decision GH-10-88, August 1989, p.1.

6. Andre Picard, "James Bay II," *The Amicus Journal*, Fall 1990.

7. *In the Matter of Canada's Landing Requirement for Pacific Coast Salmon and Herring* (Canada-US Trade Commission Panel, October 16, 1989, 2TCT 7162).

8. Letter to the Editor, *Toronto Globe and Mail*, October 28, 1989.

9. J. Dahl, "Perilous Policy: Canada Promotes Asbestos Mining, Sells Carcinogenic Mineral Heavily in the Third World," *Wall Street Journal*, December 9, 1989.

10. A. Picard and H. Enchin, "Quebec Planning to Fight US Asbestos Ban," *Toronto Globe and Mail*, July 7, 1989.

11. For one account of Canadian activities in this regard, see *Environmental Matters* (Industry's Guide to the Issues, the Challenges, and the Solutions), June 1990, EM10.

Economics for Future Generations

George Watts

I'm a Nuu-chah-nulth Indian. I live on the same piece of soil that my great, great, great, great grandfather lived on. I have not moved one inch from where we lived.

I don't think our position in Canada is any different than any other people that have been colonized by the Europeans, and I believe it is appropriate to start to set the record straight because in 1992 a number of countries are going to celebrate that we were colonized. And I don't see those issues as being any different than the Free Trade Agreement. It ultimately ends up in the oppression of people.

So what is going on? Why did we have Canadian-American free trade? Why do they want American-Mexican or American-Mexican-Canadian free trade?

They want it because it is the last shot at getting wealth in this world. Everything else is coming down on them. People are starting to question the environment. There are no more places left in the world to colonize people, so they can't make wealth on colonization anymore.

And who pays the price? Well I know who. It's the people at the lowest end of the economic scale who bear all the burden. So that these guys can have their money.

Instead of offering leadership about where this world should be thirty or forty years from now, what they are saying is, "I can protect you tomorrow. But don't worry about your kids or your grandchildren, because they may end up in the sewer."

Well, I come from a different culture. I don't care about myself. I don't care what I own. I don't give a damn if I wake up tomorrow with one thing in my pocket. But I care very much about my grandchildren and where they are going to be. Think about where your grandchildren are going to be. I would suggest that if you buy into the American economy, your children are going to be guaranteed that they are going to be living in sewers. Because the people who have that wealth don't give a damn about your grandchildren.

George Watts is chief of the Nuu-Chah-Nulth Tribal Council and Chair of the Economic Development Committee of the Assembly of First Nations. This was excerpted from his speech to the 'Canada-Mexico Encuentro' on October 5, 1990 that appeared in the Pro-Canada Dossier #29 (January/February 1991).

2. Free Trade Myths

THIS MODERN WORLD by TOM TOMORROW

HEY, CITIZENS! IT'S TIME FOR YET ANOTHER EDITION OF "HOW THE NEWS WORKS"...

STEP ONE: THE PRESIDENT DESCRIBES, IN VAGUE AND GENERAL TERMS, THE BENEFITS OF A *FREE TRADE AGREEMENT* WITH *MEXICO*.

FREE ENTERPRISE! GROWTH! BLAH! BLAH! BLAH!

STEP TWO: AN ECONOMIST IS TROTTED OUT TO EXPLAIN HOW THROWING THOUSANDS OF PEOPLE OUT OF WORK WILL BE *GOOD* FOR THE *ECONOMY*.

YOU SEE, ONCE BUSINESSES ARE FREE TO MOVE OPERATIONS TO *MEXICO*...

...THEY WILL NO LONGER BE FORCED TO PAY EXHORBITANT WAGES TO AMERICAN WORKERS! CORPORATE PROFITS WILL *SOAR!* THE ECONOMY WILL *TURN AROUND!* THE RECESSION WILL *END!*

STEP THREE: POSSIBLY-- JUST POSSIBLY-- A REPORTER WILL ASK THE OBVIOUS QUESTION...

...BUT--WHAT WILL HAPPEN TO ALL THE WORKERS WHO LOSE THEIR *JOBS* ?

OH, NO PROBLEM--THEY'LL BE RETRAINED!

STEP FOUR: DOUBTS THUS ASSUAGED BY GLIB REASSURANCES, THE MAINSTREAM NEWS MEDIA FALLS DUTIFULLY INTO LINE...

--AND AFTER ALL--WHAT'S GOOD FOR *BUSINESS* IS GOOD FOR *AMERICA!*

STEP FIVE: THE PRESIDENT EVENTUALLY GETS HIS WAY. DISPLACED WORKERS ARE RETRAINED AND SETTLE INTO FULFILLING NEW CAREERS.

YOU WANT *FRIES* WITH THAT?

FUN MEAL®

TOM TOMORROW © '91 COMMENTS? BOX 460573 SF CA 94146

Introduction

John Gershman

If the lessons of the Canada-US FTA are sobering, the implications of a continental agreement are even more so. Advocates of the NAFTA promise a better future for all citizens of North America. This section weaves the voices and stories of the victims of free trade, with analysis that confronts head-on the paradise promised by the NAFTA's advocates.

David Brooks begins with a brief overview of recent Mexican developments, illuminating the political and economic context in which the Salinas Administration is pursuing the NAFTA. The myth that the NAFTA is just about trade is exploded by Adolfo Aguilar Zinser and the Toronto-based Ecumenical Coalition for Economic Justice. Taking a broader development perspective, they highlight how focusing exclusively on trade and investment issues ignores the crucial issues of debt, development, and democracy; issues which are critical to ensuring the widest distribution of benefits from continental integration.

The myth that free trade will lead to higher wages in both Mexico and the US is tackled by Richard Rothstein, who demonstrates that this claim is at odds with the reality of US-Mexico relations. Rothstein shows that since most trade is already 'free' between the US and Mexico, the NAFTA will encourage US and Canadian firms to move to Mexico and exploit lower wages and environmental standards, while coercing workers into taking wage cutbacks in the US and Canada. Nor will the influx of new investment in Mexico lead to dramatic increases in the standard of living of Mexican workers, already ravaged by a decade of structural adjustment programs. One factor is that the destruction of small-scale subsistence agriculture and domestic-oriented Mexican firms will increase the labor pool, keeping wages low. Another is represented in the experiences of Vicente Guerrero, as described by Matt Moffett – the reliance by many transnational corporations and Mexican firms on exploiting child labor.

As the maquildora plants are likely to expand rapidly under free trade, they deserve some special discussion. Originally plants that assembled imported components for re-export to the US, predominantly textile and garment factories, they now include microelectronics, food processing, and automobile plants. Having moved beyond simple assembly operations, the productivity of Mexican workers now approaches that of US workers, with much lower wages and environmental standards – a strong incentive for firms to move south of the Rio Grande. The living and working conditions of the overwhelmingly female workforce are described by Sandy Tolan, Jerry Kramer, and the words of one anonymous maquila worker.

In response to demands by environmental groups that environmental standards be enforced, and in an attempt to divide the NAFTA's opponents, the Bush Administration released an environmental action plan in May 1991. The inadequacies of the plan led all but a few groups to continue to press for integrated environmental and economic agreements, and to demand specific funding be provided for a border clean-up program, as well as to assist the Mexican government in implementing their environmental regulations. David Ortman draws on the European Community experience to indicate the probable global and regional impact of the NAFTA, while Rodney Leonard and Eric Christensen indicate how, as presently proposed, it will be an environmental disaster – pushing environmental regulations to the lowest common denominator. The National Toxics Campaign report illustrates how low that common denominator is, exposing the environmental and public health costs that free trade has already wrought.

Mark Ritchie and Jorge Calderon Salazar discuss how the NAFTA will benefit chemical intensive, large-scale agribusiness and undermine both the Mexican subsistence agriculture sector as well as family farms in the US, sectors essential to sustainable farming practices and food security.

Different aspects of the struggle for democracy are discussed by contributors addressing the human rights situation in Mexico, and the probable impact of NAFTA on Mexican immigration to the US. While John Burstein discusses the need for human rights to be a central item on the agenda if the NAFTA is not to entrench authoritarianism in Mexico, Mariclare Acosta demonstrates how human rights and democracy are intricately related in Mexico.

Recent reports issued by Americas Watch and Amnesty International have exposed the serious human rights violations occurring against Mexican immigrants in the US. The NAFTA, notes Arnoldo García, will serve to exacerbate violations by not providing specific protection for immigrants and migrant workers. Jorge Castañeda and Rafael Alarcon discuss how the NAFTA's failure to address immigration issues head-on will actually undermine the widest possible distribution of benefits and promote the exploitation of unprotected Mexican labor in the US.

The fatal flaws of the proposed NAFTA outlined by the contributors to this section illustrate that the promises of free trade are false promises – a paradise indeed, but an exclusive paradise for the privileged few.

Mexico: The Forgotten Neighbor

Mexico's Future Hinges On Political and Economic Reforms

David Brooks

In 1982 Mexico's economy ceased to grow for the first time since the 1930s. Political stability in Mexico had always depended on sustained economic growth; without it the entire system was thrown into crisis.

By the 1970s, contradictions inherent in Mexico's spectacular economic growth, most of them rooted in the industrialization model of the 1950s, began to tear the system apart. The ever-shrinking buying power of the majority of people limited the domestic market and ultimately production; persistent requirements for foreign capital and technology created a constant balance-of-payments deficit; and the growing fiscal deficit impaired the state's ability to blunt the social effects of these economic disparities. The discovery of new oil deposits in 1976 was heralded as the savior of the economy – the solution to debt, unemployment, and capital scarcity in the short term; the path out of underdevelopment in the long term. But instead of rescuing the economy, oil merely hastened its collapse.

To develop the oil industry and convert it into the engine for a new (though brief) era of unparalleled prosperity, Mexico required vast new loans, and international bankers were most obliging. The debt accumulated in the 1970s, (from $4.5 billion in 1971 to $19.6 billion by 1976) and then increased four-fold (to over $80 billion) again by 1982. The sharp drop in the price of oil in mid-1981 through 1982 and the deteriorating world market for many Mexican exports teamed up with other internal factors to assault the Mexican economy.

Between 1982 and 1988 the administration of Miguel del la Madrid and the long-ruling Partido Revolucionario Institucional (PRI) applied an International Monetary Fund-designed austerity program to confront the economic crisis and guarantee payments on Mexico's $108 billion foreign debt.

The program's social costs included a combined under- and unemployment rate of 50 percent of the labor force, malnourishment of over half the population, and poverty for some 40 million of the country's 85 million people in one of the wealthiest economies of the developing world. For the majority of Mexicans, the medicine to cure the crisis only made it worse.

On July 6, 1988, a political earthquake struck the nation: a massive vote for progressive opposition presidential candidate Cuauhtémoc Cárdenas, leader of a center-left coalition. The ruling PRI party and its entrenched state apparatus reacted with panic. The computer vote-counting system was declared 'down,' and during the next week an unprecedented fraud was carried out. PRI candidate Carlos Salinas was declared the winner with only an official 51 percent majority. At the same time, mounting evidence of the electoral fraud emerged, including altered ballots and packets of burned opposition ballots. The government refuses to this day to recount some 45 percent of the votes, and the legitimacy of the Salinas government has been in question ever since.

Cárdenas – a former PRI governor and congressman and son of Mexico's most revered post-revolutionary president, Lazaro Cárdenas (1943-40) – along with a number of other renowned PRI members, had tried to reform the party from within during 1987. After this futile effort, Cárdenas launched his presidential campaign and today is the most important national opposition leader in Mexico. Cárdenas calls for full implementation of the progressive measures and democratic procedures framed in the still-standing Mexican Revolution's 1917 constitution, redirection of economic policy to meet the basic needs of the majority of Mexicans, and the end of the PRI's 60-year monopoly of the political system. Cárdenas' coalition, now solidified into an opposition party, Partido de la Revolución Democrática (PRD), was sparked by grassroots peasant, labor, student, and popular urban movements that grew in response to the repressive economic policies of the de la Madrid administration (1982-88).

Carlos Salinas, a Harvard-educated economist, established his presidency on a platform to 'modernize' Mexico through acceleration of de la Madrid's neo-liberal economic policies: privatization of the majority of publicly owned enterprises, aggressive promotion of foreign investment, massive support of the export sector of the economy, and designation of private development. The president and his cabinet ministers, mostly foreign-trained technocrats with limited political experience, are convinced that these policies are the only realistic approach to launching Mexico into the world economy of the 1990s.

One aspect of its modernization policy, according to the government, includes democratic reforms of the political system. Even though there have been efforts toward this – such as recognizing the conservative PAN party's governorship in Baja California and several local opposition victories in mayoral and congressional elections – continuing electoral fraud and increasing repression of opposition movements raise serious doubts about these highly touted political reforms. More than 90 PRD members have been killed in election-related violence since the 1988 elections, and human rights violations have become a predominant issue today.

Mexico's immediate political future will be shaped by the mobilization of opposition political movements as well as by the success or failure of the Salinas economic program, and here the US plays a pivotal role. Mexico's relations with Washington are of paramount importance for the success of the Salinas program and, in fact, for the future of the government's stability in Mexico. The US is Mexico's largest foreign investor, trading partner, and creditor. Mexico is the US' third largest trading partner, a strategic source of foreign oil, and Mexico offers a vast reserve of some of the world's lowest paid labor. The economic integration process between the two countries that has been going on over the last eight years will be, Salinas hopes, formalized through the current negotiations for a free trade agreement. Maquiladoras factories along the border are the leading edge of economic integration and continue to be Mexico's most dynamic economic sector, second only to oil in providing foreign exchange. Critics point out that this integration process continues to rapidly erode Mexico's sovereignty through dramatically increasing dependence on the North.

Yet, the key issue in Mexico still remains: the government's response to the call for wide-spread democratization of both the political and the economic system. With Cárdenas expected to challenge the ruling party again in the 1994 presidential elections, it is clear that these are the issues that will determine Mexico's future.

David Brooks is director of the US-Mexico Diálogos. He wrote this article for the Utne Reader *(November/December 1990).*

Free Trade: Prosperity for the Few or Development for the Majority?

Adolfo Aguilar Zinser

Free trade must be above all an instrument of prosperity. Without the social development dimension discussed below, the North American Free Trade Agreement (NAFTA) will at best serve only to promote economic growth restricted to the northern regions of Mexico, where the economic integration with the US is really taking place. This will happen at the expense of regional development and economic equity in most of the country. Instead of boosting Mexico's overall economic and social development, the agreement will help to concentrate income in few hands and in few places, jeopardize the environment, and restrict economic opportunities. Ultimately it will promote the consolidation of the authoritarian, anti-democratic system of government suffered by Mexico. Such an agreement would endanger the future of US-Mexican cooperation and friendship.

Negotiating a comprehensive pact does not mean that we indiscriminately include all aspects of our relationship, but rather, only those related to trade and development. Mexico is not a democracy, and not even the best and most comprehensive NAFTA can modify that. Only Mexicans can change the authoritarian regime. However, the discussion as well as the completion of a fair and equitable trade pact with the US and Canada can help Mexicans in their struggle for economic rights and civil liberties.

The majority of Mexicans are not opposed 'in principle' to the NAFTA. In fact, never before has Mexican society been better inclined to negotiate a broad economic agreement with the US than today. Opinion surveys and public discussions show very clearly that most Mexicans share the hope that a NAFTA will bring necessary economic changes to our relations with the US and new opportunities for the country and its people. However, concerned Mexican citizens are opposed to the authoritarian methods by which the government wants to resolve this issue. There is in Mexico a growing fear that in the process of these negotiations some fundamental social concerns will be ignored, and that Mexican authorities, urged by their own short-term political necessities, will make costly concessions and sign a bad deal when a mutually beneficial agreement is possible.

These suspicions refer mainly to three fundamental questions. First and foremost is the fear that oil resources will be traded in the agreement for commercial concessions or investment commitments. Oil has a central role in Mexico's modern struggle for independence; it is not only a symbol of sovereignty, it is widely recognized as a collective patrimony, a resource Mexicans should use responsibly for development, and should preserve for future generations. No other national asset has this prominence. Although many Mexicans recognize that our national oil industry has not been administered prudently and efficiently, I am convinced that Mexican society is not and will never be prepared to give up this responsibility by transferring the administration of the oil industry partially or totally to private and foreign interests. The Mexican government has acknowledged these concerns and has assured the Mexican public that oil is definitely not on the

NAFTA agenda. However, not even the most energetic commitments of the authorities has dissipated public suspicions.

The second area of public suspicion relates to the fear that the NAFTA will only benefit a few industrial, commercial, and financial monopolies who control most of Mexico's assets and wealth. The past few years prove that economic liberalization and privatization are not necessarily conducive to the decentralization of political and economic power. Free trade might displace small and medium-sized industries, leaving the industrial and commercial base of the country in the hands of big sharks and foreign investors. In any event, most Mexicans are aware of the fact that market-oriented economic policies are not adopted in Mexico at the expense of the government's power to impose arbitrarily its will on economic actors. Wage controls that have cost a 60 percent reduction of real income since 1982 are a vivid example of how the government combines economic freedom with political imposition. As long as the investment promotion policies of the government are based on low wages, and while independent and democratic unions continue to be suppressed, Mexican workers know that salaries will not increase when jobs are created nor when productivity rises. A social charter and an effective dispute settlement mechanism authorized by the agreement to hear their demands would reassure Mexican workers that the purpose of the continental economic pact is *really* to close the gap gradually between the rich and poor.

The third major concern expressed by the Mexican public is the future of Mexico's subsistence agriculture. This is not a sector like any other: it will require outright protection and significant support for an indefinite period of time. The social consequences and the migratory effect of suddenly exposing it to indiscriminate international competition would be simply disastrous for ten million people and our two countries.

The difference between the restricted agreement currently being negotiated and an agreement built around social and development preoccupations is not between a realistic, viable one, as opposed to an unattainable, idealistic one. The difference is the extent to which free trade will be used to secure the privileges already enjoyed by a few economic interests, instead of being a bridge to close income gaps between Mexico and the US. The difference is simply between a bad deal and a fair and promising continental development pact.

Adolfo Aguilar Zinser is a professor and senior researcher at the Center for Studies of the United States of the National Autonomous University of Mexico (UNAM). This is excerpted from his testimony to the Subcommittee on International Economic Policy and Trade and the Subcommittee on Western Hemispheric Affairs of the US House Foreign Affairs Committee, March 6, 1991.

Free Trade Won't Help Mexico's Poor

Ecumenical Coalition for Economic Justice

Canadian Prime Minister Brian Mulroney has resorted to a hackneyed saying from the 1960s, 'trade not aid', to defend a North American Free Trade Agreement (NAFTA). Mulroney wants Canadians to think that free trade will benefit Mexico's poor.

Mexican President Carlos Salinas de Gortari says Mexico wants "to export goods, not people," warning that without free trade, "Instead of seeing hundreds of thousands of Mexicans crossing the border looking for jobs in the north, you will see millions." Salinas invited Canadian and American firms to invest in Mexico and take advantage of low wage labor to compete with Europe and Japan.

Salinas claims that a free trade deal will allow Mexican incomes "to recover on a permanent basis." But will it? Is the real aim to improve conditions for Mexican workers? Or will they be doomed to remain a low-wage labor force at the service of a continental corporate elite?

There are at least three reasons why a NAFTA will not lead to rising living standards for the majority of Mexicans: debt, demographic growth, and rural depopulation.

Debt

Since 1982 more than half of Mexico's international trade earnings have been handed over to foreign banks to cover interest payments on its foreign debt. Mexico has turned itself inside out in an effort to increase export earnings. The structural adjustment programs imposed by foreign creditors have involved devaluation of the peso, unilateral lowering of import barriers, severe wage controls, high interest rates, deep cuts in government spending, privatization of state enterprises, and changes in foreign investment regulations.

The effects of structural adjustment have been devastating for Mexico's poor. Real wages fell over 60 percent. Thousands of peasant farmers lost their land. Over 700,000 jobs disappeared from Mexican industry. Wealthy Mexicans invested so much in US banks and real estate that their holdings are now estimated to be worth as much as Mexico's entire external debt.

Despite all these sacrifices and despite the modest amount of debt relief received under the US-sponsored Brady Plan, Mexico still had to hand over some US$9 billion in interest payments to its creditors in 1990.

The US initiative to negotiate a NAFTA is part of a strategy to make permanent the structural adjustments forced on Mexico by its foreign creditors. Increased exports – whether of petroleum, tomatoes, or the value added by Mexican labor to North American products assembled in the maquiladoras – are crucial to keeping a net flow of wealth into the coffers of Northern banks. Little of the income that Mexico might earn through increased North American trade is likely to be available for domestic investment as long as Mexico has to make its onerous debt servicing obligations.

Mexico's structural adjustment has transformed the country into a haven for foreign investors seeking low-wage labor. The cost of employing a young woman to assemble products in a maquiladora fell from US$1.53 an hour in 1982 to just 60 cents in 1990. Mexican labor costs employers less than one quarter of what they would pay in Hong Kong, Taiwan, or Singapore.

Defenders of a NAFTA argue that it will raise Mexican wages and living standards over time. But this position ignores several crucial factors. There is no free collective bargaining between Mexican unions and employers. The corrupt trade union movement, linked to the government party, has accepted wage pacts far below the rate of inflation as part of Mexico's structural adjustment while independent union movements are severely repressed. The economic growth model promoted by Salinas depends on continued low wages. If salaries were to rise, investors would simply look elsewhere for cheaper labor.

Demographic Growth

Mexico has a very young population. Forty percent of its 85 million people are under 15 years of age. Officially one million young people enter the labor force every year. As many as 10 million children work illegally. Employers skirt the law by accepting easily falsified photocopies of birth certificates when they hire 14- and 15-year-olds. Other children sell gum, wash car windows, or shine shoes to survive.

To get an idea of how rapidly this young labor force outgrows new job opportunities, one need only look at what happened between 1985 and March of 1990. The most dynamic sector, the maquiladoras, hired 242,000 new workers, while domestic industry took on just 33,513 new employees. Since maquiladoras buy only 1.7 percent of their inputs from within Mexico, few spin-off jobs are created when they expand. Total new employment over five years was less than half the number of new entrants to the labor force each year.

Rural Depopulation

Over the last 30 years some nine million *campesinos* (peasant farmers) have been forced off their land. This rural exodus occurred, in part, because large landowners turned to cattle grazing or agribusiness production of fruits and vegetables for export. In recent years the migration from rural areas has grown as crop prices have fallen by 50 percent in real terms. Government programs of technical and financial assistance to farmers have been dismantled as part of the structural adjustment program. High interest rates and the withdrawal of government credits have been devastating for Mexican farmers. All these factors have accelerated the exodus from the countryside.

Mexican *campesinos* are already suffering from their government's unilateral trade liberalization measures. After Salinas became Planning Minister in 1985, he undertook to lower tariffs and remove most items from import licensing requirements. As a result, Mexico now imports 10 million tons of agricultural products annually, equivalent to one third of its food consumption. The import bill would be higher were it not for the fact that per capita consumption of basic foods has fallen by 30 percent over the last eight years, due to the 60 percent decline in real wages and high urban unemployment.

If agricultural trade is included in a NAFTA, large landholders will gobble up more small farms. More of the best lands will be handed over to agribusiness maquiladoras using foreign capital and inputs to grow fruits and vegetables for export. Dependence on food imports would rise.

Conclusion

A NAFTA would tend to make permanent the export-oriented model imposed on Mexico by its structural adjustment program. Mexico's creditors, including Canadian banks, would continue to collect interest on loans that probably will never be repaid.

The kind of investment that would take place in Mexico would chiefly come from transnational corporations seeking to use cheap labor to produce for export since the depressed wages of Mexican workers make the domestic market unattractive.

Some new job creation would no doubt occur. But even the most optimistic economic growth projections based on an inflow of new foreign investment that might be attracted by a NAFTA would not begin to create enough jobs to absorb those currently unemployed, let alone the new entrants to the labor force and the huge numbers of peasant farmers and their families displaced from their ancestral lands by free trade in agriculture.

As Professor Adolfo Aguilar Zinser of Mexico's National Autonomous University told a Canadian parliamentary committee, "a very clear, conscious technocratic decision" has been made by Salinas and his advisors to include only half of Mexico's population in a dynamic process of economic growth. The economic model they have chosen means that by the year 2000, 50 million Mexicans would be left to languish as a reserve of cheap labor assuring that wages remain low for years to come.

Fortunately there are alternatives. Instead of pursuing a NAFTA as proposed by the Bush administration, opposition groups in Mexico are proposing development alternatives that begin by addressing Mexico's real problems.

A real alternative must include the cancellation of most of Mexico's external debt and an end to the onerous structural adjustment condition imposed by external creditors. Revitalizing small and medium Mexican industries producing for the domestic market is the key to job creation.

Authentic development for Mexico would reject free trade in agriculture and instead provide peasant farmers with adequate credits, crop insurance, marketing facilities, and fair prices to make Mexicans once again capable of feeding themselves.

Canadians wishing to stand in solidarity with poor Mexicans will join them in rejecting a NAFTA. Our best solidarity with Mexico would be to cancel the foreign debt and remove the structural adjustment conditions.

The Ecumenical Council for Economic Justice is a project of Canadian churches working for global economic justice. This appeared in the Economic Justice Report *Volume II, Number 2, May 1991.*

Workers

Free Trade Scam
Richard Rothstein

Advocates of a North American Free Trade Agreement (NAFTA) assume that US exports will grow as a result of moving labor-intensive production to developing nations because, they assert, Third World wages and purchasing power will increase with the growth of foreign investment. As evidence, the US administration points to recent growth in exports of consumer products to Mexico.

It is true that US firms have expanded sales in Mexico of toothpaste, diapers, cameras, clothing, and other consumer products since Mexican import restrictions were dropped and tariffs lowered. Yet expectations that such growth can continue are unrealistic. The Mexican middle class is tiny. With average wages under $2 an hour, relatively few Mexicans can shop for any but the most basic consumer products. Soon, the pent-up demand of this Mexican middle-class will be satisfied. Unless the incomes of Mexican workers increase dramatically, the Mexican consumer market will not boost US exports as the administration hopes.

According to free trade advocates, however, Mexican workers' wages will rise. As Mexico's industrial capacity grows (because of increased US investment and access to US markets), competition for scarce skilled and semi-skilled manufacturing labor will increase the demand for labor, raising wages. Economies of scale (from serving US markets) and greater capital investment in technology will then lead to increased Mexican factory productivity. Wages will increase as workers demand a higher share of this productivity.

Reality will be less rosy. Mexico has so enormous a pool of unemployed and underemployed workers – estimates range from 30 to 70 percent – that tightening labor markets will not cause a general increase in wage levels. And with greater economic integration, the surplus labor pool could increase rather than shrink, because many subsistence Mexican farmers will be unable to compete once Mexican agricultural protections are dismantled. Peasants' displacement could be exacerbated as agribusiness purchases their collective farmland for the production of labor-intensive vegetable crops. Rural workers, flooding industrial labor markets, will depress wages, offsetting any labor market tightening from increased investment.

Expectations that increased Mexican industrial productivity will lead to higher wages are also more likely to be realized in economics textbooks than in reality. Mexican automobile-engine plants, for example, now operate at 80 percent of US productivity rates, yet wages in these plants are only six percent of US wages rates. This is also characteristic of export plants throughout the Third World, where productivity gains have not been matched by wage increases. In Mexico itself, real wages have fallen by 50 percent in the last decade, simultaneous with increases in industrial productivity.

In the US in the 1980s, real wages fell as industrial productivity climbed, while in Japan and most European industrialized nations, productivity and wages rose together. Contrary to assertions by academic economists, there is no necessary connection between wages and economic growth, because wages are affected more by government's fiscal, monetary, and labor policies than by factory productivity.

Mexican wages have fallen in the last decade because the Mexican government, in desperate need of export earnings to repay a $100-billion foreign debt, adopted policies to attract investors in export plants by promising ever lower wages. Mexican policy could not allow wages to rise, for rising incomes would supply domestic peso purchasing power to compete with dollar earning exporters for factory production. Free trade is unlikely to change this.

Meanwhile, the Bush administration urges other Latin American countries to adopt free-market, free-trade, and export-oriented policies. Bush's 'Enterprise for the Americas Initiative' seeks a Western Hemisphere free trade area, in which each country competes for US investment by promising lower wages and less regulation of capital. With adoption of these continental 'reforms,' rising wages in Mexico will become even more unlikely. If wages rise in Mexico, new investment can go farther south. US manufacturers are used to going south to reduce labor costs.

The Administration claims that high-skill, higher-wage jobs will be created in the US as a result of sending lower-skill, lower-wage jobs to Mexico. Low-wage industrialization in Mexico, they believe, will require imports of US capital goods and high-tech services – industrial machinery, technology, computers, and software.

Yet to the extent that low-wage industry simply moves from US to Mexican locations, the gain for US capital-goods suppliers is nil. High-tech employment in the US is not enhanced if robot sales are lost to a manufacturer in Los Angeles but gained to a manufacturer in Chihuahua. A gain in US machinery sales will only come if transnational investment is shifted from Asian nations to Mexico, where factories are more likely to use American than Japanese equipment.

But shifts will likely be minimal. Most transnational investors who target US markets from Mexico rather than Asia already do so because of Mexico's proximity. Even were an FTA to stimulate additional relocations, US capital-goods exporters would gain little. The US has already lost many industrial-machinery markets to Japanese and European exporters. For example, FTA proponents expect the most rapid growth in Mexico's apparel industry, as clothing plants relocate from both the US and Asia. But the US is no longer a manufacturer of sewing, weaving, or knitting machines. Japanese, West German, and Swiss firms supply these machines throughout the world. The US apparel-machinery industry is now almost entirely reduced to the production of spare parts for the aging machine stock of US clothiers whose equipment was modern 30 years ago.

In the last decade, the US has followed policies designed to shift low-wage manufacturing to Third World locations. A Mexico FTA joins the Caribbean Basin Initiative (which goes beyond an FTA, actually subsidizing the relocation of US factories to island nations); 'foreign aid' programs (which also often include subsidies for creating export industries); International Monetary Fund and World Bank programs and the Baker and Brady debt plans (all of which require low-wage policies and the suppression of domestic consumption as part of debt-repayment schemes); and US leadership in the GATT, the General Agreement on Tariffs and Trade, which pushes on a worldwide basis policies similar to the FTA. At each step of the way, the administration and its academic economists have predicted a gain in US wealth and employment as a result of increased trade and mobility of investment.

Yet the gains don't seem to materialize. Manufacturing's share of US employment fell from 23 percent to 18 percent in the 1980s. The 1.5 million lost manufacturing jobs were mostly replaced not by robot designers and software writers but by retail and low-wage service workers. The median weekly pay of US manufacturing workers is over $400; for service workers it is $350 and for retail workers $275. Partly as a result of our deindustrialization and free-trade policies, the share of income going to the top fifth of American families went up, while the share going to the bottom three-fifths declined. More US investment in Mexico's low-wage export sector will not likely reverse these trends; it will intensify them.

With capital so much more mobile than labor, unrestrained free-trade policies have led to declining fortunes not only of Third World populations but of most Americans as well. More surprising is that Americans so easily accept a wildly unrealistic *international* laissez-faire ideology, when similar dogmas have long been discredited at home. For example, despite battles over the *level* of the domestic minimum wage, most Americans accept its logic. Few believe that Californians would benefit if Mississippi were permitted to lure manufacturing plants by lowering Mississippi's minimum wages to $1 an hour. Yet when Chihuahua makes an identical offer, otherwise reasonable people (even Democratic politicians) start dreaming about software sales to Mexico. California Governor Pete Wilson warned that businesses might abandon California if the state's personal income tax were raised by a mere seven-tenths of one percent on incomes over $100,000. Yet the same Governor Wilson favors a Mexican free trade agreement, which encourages businesses to leave California for Mexico in quest of minimal taxes, little environmental regulation, and payroll savings of 85 percent.

Richard Rothstein is a research associate with the Economic Policy Institute. This is excerpted from his article of the same title in the LA Weekly, *May 17, 1991.*

Working Children
Matt Moffett
When Vicente Guerrero reported to work at the shoe factory, he had to leave his yo-yo with the guard at the door. Then Vicente, who had just turned 12 years old, was led to his post on the assembly line: a tall vertical lever attached to a press that bonds the soles of sneakers to the uppers.

The lever was set so high that Vicente had to shinny up the press and throw all his 90 pounds backward to yank the stiff steel bar downward. It reminded him of some playground contraption. For Vicente this would have to pass for recreation from now on. A recent graduate of the sixth grade, he joined a dozen other children working full time in the factory. Once the best orator in the school and a good student, he now learned the wisdom of silence: even opening his mouth in this poorly ventilated plant meant breathing poisonous fumes.

Vicente's journey from the front-row desk of his schoolroom to the factory assembly line was charted by adults: impoverished parents, a heedless employer, hapless regulators, and impotent educators. "I figure work must be good for me, because many older people have helped put me here," says Vicente, shaking his hair out of his big, dark eyes. "And in the factory I get to meet lots of other boys."

Half of Mexico's 85 million people are below the age of 18, and this generation has been robbed of its childhood by a decade of debt crisis. It's illegal in Mexico to hire children under 14, but the Mexico City Assembly recently estimated that anywhere from five to ten million children are employed illegally, often in hazardous jobs. "Economic necessity is stronger than a theoretical prohibition," says Alfredo Farit Rodriguez, Mexico's Attorney General in Defense of Labor, a kind of workers' ombudsman.

Little Foxes

Young Vicente Guerrero's life exemplifies both the poverty that forces children to seek work and the porous regulatory system that makes it all too easy for them to find jobs. In the shantytown where Vicente lives, and throughout the central Mexico state of Guanajuato, it is customary for small and medium-sized factories to employ boy shoemakers known as *zorritas*, or little foxes.

"My father says I was lucky to have so many years to be lazy before I went to work," says Vicente. His father, Patricio Guerrero, entered the shoe factories of Guanajuato at the age of seven. Three decades of hard work later, Mr. Guerrero lives in a tumbledown brick shell about the size and shape of a baseball dugout. It is home to 25 people, maybe 26. Mr. Guerrero himself isn't sure how many relatives and family friends are currently lodged with him, his wife, and six children. Vicente, to get some privacy in the bedroom he shares with eight other children, occasionally rigs a crude tent from the laundry on the clotheslines crisscrossing the hut.

School was the one place Vicente had no problem settling himself apart from other kids. Classmates, awed by his math skills, called him "the wizard." Nearly as adept in other subjects, Vicente finished first among 105 sixth-graders in a general-knowledge exam.

Vicente's academic career reached its zenith during a speaking contest he won last June on the last day of school. The principal was so moved by the patriotic poem he recited that she called him into her office to repeat it just for her. That night, Vicente told his family the whole story. He spoke of how nervous he had been on the speaker's platform and how proud he was to sit on the principal's big stuffed chair.

After he finished, there was a strained silence. "Well," his father finally said, "it seems that you've learned everything that you can in school." Mr. Guerrero then laid his plans for Vicente's next lesson in life. In a few weeks, there would be an opening for Vicente at Deportes Mike, the athletic shoe factory where Mr. Guerrero himself had just been hired. Vicente would earn 100,000 pesos a week, about $34.

Last August Vicente was introduced to the Deportes Mike assembly line. About a dozen of the 50 workers were underage boys, many of whom toiled alongside their fathers. One youth, his cheek bulging with sharp tacks, hammered at some baseball shoes. A tiny 10-year-old was napping in a crate that he should have been filling with shoe molds. A bigger boy was running a stamping machine he had decorated with decals of Mickey Mouse and Tinker Bell. The bandage wrapped around the stamper's hand gave Vicente an uneasy feeling.

Showing Vicente the ropes was the plant superintendent's 13- year-old son, Francisco Guerrero, a cousin of Vicente's who was a toughened veteran with three years experience in shoemaking.

When a teacher came by the factory to chide school dropouts, Francisco rebuked her. "I'm earning 180,000 pesos a week," he said. "What do you make?" The teacher, whose weekly salary is 120,000 pesos, could say nothing.

Vicente's favorite part of his new job is running the clanking press, though that usually occupies a small fraction of his eight-hour workday. He spends most of his time on dirtier work: smearing glue onto the soles of shoes with his hands. The can of glue he dips his fingers into is marked "toxic substances ... prolonged or repeated inhalation causes grave health damage; do not leave in the reach of minors." All the boys ignore the warning.

Impossible to ignore is the sharp, sickening odor of the glue. The only ventilation in the factory is from slits in the wall where bricks were removed, and from a window near Vicente that opens only halfway. Just a matter of weeks after he started working, Vicente was home in bed with a cough, burning eyes and nausea.

What provoked Vicente's illness, according to the doctor he saw at the public hospital, was the glue fumes. Ingredients aren't listed on the label, but the glue's manufacturer, Simon S.A. of Mexico City, says it contains toluene, a petroleum extract linked to liver, lung, and central nervous system damage. The maximum exposure to toluene permitted under Mexican environmental law is twice the level recommended by recently tightened US standards. And in any event, Deportes Mike's superintendent doesn't recall a government health inspector coming around in the nine years the plant has been open.

When Vicente felt well enough to return to work a few days later, a fan was installed near his machine. "The smell still makes you choke," Vicente says, "but *el patrón* says I'll get used to it."

El patrón, the factory owner, is Alfredo Hidalgo. "These kinds of problems will help make a man of him," Mr. Hidalgo says. "It's a tradition here that boys grow up quickly." Upholding tradition has been good for Mr. Hidalgo's business: Vicente and the other zorritas generally are paid less than adult workers.

Mr. Hidalgo doesn't see that as exploitation. "If it were bad for Vicente, he wouldn't have come back after the first day of work," he says. "None of the boys would, and my company wouldn't be able to survive."

Matt Moffett is a staff reporter for The Wall Street Journal. *This is excerpted from his article in the April 8, 1991 issue .*

Maquiladoras

Life in the Low-Wage Boomtowns of Mexico

Sandy Tolan with Jerry Kammer

Nogales, Sonora

At five o'clock on a December morning, in a two-room shack standing adjacent to a strip of American-owned factories, the cold touches the faces of seven young Mexicans, asleep for the moment under mounds of covers. One by one, this family has come north from the small town of Navajo in central Mexico. Work in the vegetable fields around Navajo has dwindled, so the lure of the factories along the Mexican-US border, eight hours to the north, is strong.

Juanita Rodriguez, 24 years old, crawls from under the blankets, dresses quickly, and prepares for another day at the garage door opener factory. Her brothers and sisters still sleep: Rosalinda, home from the night shift at the sewing factory; José, soon to begin another day at the carburetor factory; Pancho, looking for work at the vegetable packing houses on the US side of the line; his wife, Leticia, pregnant, and until recently working at the sunglasses assembly plant. Juanita leaves them all to their dreams. The shack that the Rodriguez family calls home was built by Juanita and her brothers from materials discarded by the nearby factories. Wooden pallets became the frame and roof. Cardboard boxes, used to ship garage door opener parts into Mexico, are now the family's interior walls. The Rodriguezes fastened the cardboard to the frame by driving nails through bottle caps. Juanita bought some glass for a window, found a door, made a picket fence of pallets.

Looming above the Rodriguez shack like a fortress is the garage door opener factory. The Chamberlain Group of Chicago built this big, new factory in 1988 with profits from their 17 years of making garage door openers in Mexico and shipping them to the US.

Every day, thousands of garage door openers come off the assembly line in Nogales, bound for Sears stores north of the border. The $149 retail price is equal to a day's wage for 20 of the company's 1,500 assembly line workers. Chamberlain saves millions of dollars a year in labor costs and has captured the garage door opener market in the US.

"We are the cost leader in our industry," says Chamberlain vice president Ray McMinn. "And we believe our location in Mexico has enabled us to achieve that status."

Juanita, who started at Chamberlain's plant six years ago, now makes one of the top factory wages in town: the peso equivalent of $7.50 a day, plus two meals. That comes to $38 a week for 48 hours of work.

When Juanita came north on the bus from Navajo at age 18, she hoped the factory work would be a stepping stone to college and a career as a nurse. But heading for work on this cold morning in December, Juanita is no closer to her dream than she was in 1983. "Our salaries are only enough to buy food, clothes, and shoes," Juanita says matter-of-factly. "Sometimes we make enough to make ends meet; sometimes we don't."

On the floor of the Chamberlain garage door opener factory, as the company executives take me on a tour of the plant, I stop behind a young woman sitting among a long row of other workers. She stares down the conveyor as a shiny black chassis slides into place. She grasps an electric air gun, presses a switch, and spins a tiny metal bolt into place. She repeats this operation every nine seconds. At this rate, she will spin 3,480 bolts by the end of the day.

One cold afternoon, I stop by to visit the Rodriguezes. Juanita isn't back from the garage door opener factory yet, but Leticia and her cousin Pedro are home, sitting on the kitchen chairs in their winter coats, listening to *norteño* music on the radio.

Leticia makes coffee on a small camping stove. Eighteen and pregnant with her second child, Leticia had just quit work at the Foster Grant factory in the *parque industrial*. Her husband, Pancho, has temporary work at a discount retailer across the border in Nogales, Arizona. Rosalinda has just left for the night shift at Kimberly-Clark.

"You suffer a lot here to earn a little more," Leticia says, pulling her old down jacket tightly around her neck. Back home she picked vegetables for a while. The pay was worse, but most things were less expensive than on the border.

Here, the family does most of its shopping at the Safeway on the US side. A lot of items – chicken, milk, even beans – are cheaper over there. Still, to buy a chicken, Leticia must work half a day. Two hours of work on the assembly line will buy a toothbrush. Even a pound of beans is equal to an hour's work in a maquila. An extra pair of shoes, a magazine, a soda, a ticket to the movies – these are luxuries.

"We came with the idea that things would be better," Leticia says. "But I don't see anything better here. *Nothing.*"

Leticia unrolls her curlers, combs out her long, black hair, looks into a pocket mirror, applies some eyeliner. She stops, squints, looks at me with a question in her eyes.

"Is it sad like this on the other side, too?"

Sandy Tolan is co-director of Desert West News *and Jerry Kammer is an investigative reporter with the* Arizona Republic. *This was excerpted from an article that appeared in the* Utne Reader *No. 42, (November/December 1990) that originally appeared in the* Tucson Weekly *(October 18, 1989).*

They Won't Pay for My Hands

Sandra Arenal, translated by Carolyn Bancroft

"I am 22 years old and I've been working in the maquiladoras for six years. I have lasted longer than the others," she tells us as she shows us her hands – deformed fingers and with an enormous, tannish-yellowish corn on each of her thumbs which extends from the tip down to the palm. When she sees our expressions she adds, "This is the cost of working here.

"Since I have entered I have been in the same department ... I get minimum wage and I do what appears to be very simple. The company is called Hamill de Mexico; we manufacture seat belts for the rear seats of cars, for Fords and Dodges I think. I don't know anything more than that, except that Mexican cars don't have these belts but American cars do. The belts are sent to us from Canada, and we put the clasps and buckles on.

"The strap comes to me on a conveyor belt, I must stretch it out, placing the pieces on each end, and then I must hold it with a hot iron for 20 seconds, lift up the iron, take away the belt, and begin the operation again ... As you see, it doesn't seem like much, but when you have to do five operations, like I do, in 30 seconds, with a hot machine, and 1,800 times a day, the results are this." And she shows us her hands again.

"I repeat, I am not old. I'm 22; nevertheless, I know that I'm not going to last long because my hands hurt more and more. There was a time when they were only deformed, they didn't hurt. Now the pain gets worse and worse, and furthermore, my movements are not as fast as they used to be. Therefore, in a short while they will lay me off, or, more likely, they won't renew my contract. Here one gets used to being terminated in December and in January they do new contracts, and, of course, those who are no longer useful don't get new contracts.

"That's the way it goes every year, and we know it. But what can you do?" With sadness she looks down at her hands. "They won't pay for my hands. When I've gone to the social security to ask the doctor for sick leave, or some kind of proof that the machine is hurting my hands, they have told me that the problem is hereditary, or that it is rheumatism, or that it was caused by my own negligence."

Sandra Arenal is the author of Sangre Joven: Las Maquiladoras por dentro *(Mexico City: Editorial Nuestro Tiempo, 1986), from which this is excerpted. Carolyn Bancroft works with the Third World Women's Project of the Institute for Policy Studies.*

Environment

Border Rivers in Peril

Sanford J. Lewis, Marco Kaltofen, and Gregory Ormsby
Drawn by the low costs of operations, over 1,800 maquiladora plants have been built along Mexico's northern border. The promise of jobs at these maquilas has led millions of Mexicans to migrate from rural areas to northern cities.

The La Paz Agreement, signed by the US and Mexico in 1983, requires that all industries that import chemicals to Mexico ship any resulting wastes back to the country of origin. Yet according to 1988 Environmental Protection Agency records, fewer than one percent of maquiladoras reported sending hazardous wastes back to the US.

In 1990, neighborhood leaders from northern Mexico asked the US-based National Toxic Campaign Fund to evaluate toxic chemical discharges in their communities. The research combined spot sampling with additional research on water quality and public policy regarding three border waterways: the Rio Grande, the New River, the Tijuana River, and the Nogales Wash).

The Rio Grande

The Rio Grande is the largest of the waterways shared by the US and Mexico. Despite the critical importance of the Rio Grande to communities on both sides of the border, the river is under siege by pollution which has already rendered tap water undrinkable in some communities.

Nuevo Laredo/Laredo Area: In Nuevo Laredo, the maquiladoras have been cited for contaminating the Rio Grande. Metals, including mercury and aluminum, have been linked to discharges from these plants. Due to the discharge of untreated and minimally treated sewage in Nuevo Laredo, the Rio Grande is unsafe for 25 miles downstream. Fecal contamination levels regularly exceed, often by a factor of a hundred, standards established to protect public health. This contaminated water is routinely drawn from the river to irrigate crops, posing a serious health threat to agricultural workers and consumers of agricultural products. Not much further down, over a million people depend for their water supply upon the ability of the waters of the Rio Grande to assimilate contaminants. In the event of a serious drought or further pollution, the Nuevo Laredo/Laredo contaminants could obstruct these downstream water uses.

Lower Rio Grande: Upwards of 98 percent of the drinking water used in the Lower Rio Grande Valley is drawn from the river. Despite the critical need to prevent any further degradation of water resources, the appalling water pollution and toxic contamination conditions indicate that this entire area is becoming a toxic disaster zone.

At the Finsa Industrial Park, Matamoros, a discharge adjacent to the Rimir automobile trim plant, whose parent corporation is General Motors, contained xylene at 2.8 million parts per billion. These levels are so high that the sample itself could be considered a hazardous waste. Xylene is a solvent which causes respiratory irritation, brain hemorrhage and other internal bleeding, lung, liver, and kidney damage.

A canal flowing through an impoverished Matamoros neighborhood contained the widest range of contaminants detected in the study. Located downstream from the discharge of the Rimir plant, toxins found in this water present a serious health threat to the residents, either through ingestion, contact with polluted water, or respiration of these volatile chemicals as they evaporate.

The New River

The New River begins in Mexico as a tiny channel draining from crops south of Mexicali. It widens as it passes through Mexicali and crosses into the US at Calexico, California, winding north through southern California's Imperial Valley and into the Salton Sea, California's largest lake.

The New River was once a place where people would escape for a day of fishing, hiking along its banks, or even a cool dip on a hot summer afternoon. Today, the New River is known as the US' dirtiest river, perhaps the most polluted stretch of river in all of North America. The river crosses the border with a thick foam, full of bacteria, industrial chemicals, and according to one EPA official, "every disease known in the western hemisphere." Over a hundred toxic pollutants have been detected in the waters of the New River, including PCB's, vinyl chloride, and other chemicals that are either acutely toxic to humans or are known carcinogens.

The pollution is so bad people are advised to not even *go near* the river. The banks have been posted with warning signs at bridges and access points throughout the length of the US side. The ecological impacts of pollution have also been severe. Toxins accumulate in the tissue of wildlife, and fish and bird kills have occurred with increasing frequency, even in the Salton Sea National Wildlife Refuge.

A large percentage of the maquiladoras in Mexicali are in industrial sectors, such as electronics and circuit board manufacture, which use hazardous substances. Of 16 volatile organic compounds known to be used in the assembly of printed circuit boards, 13 have been detected repeatedly in the water of the New River. Many of the chemicals detected are known or suspected carcinogens.

Municipal dumps in Mexicali are another source of New River contamination. Several have been built within the New River drainage basin, some directly adjacent to or even on top of New River tributaries. Mexicali industries are known to have disposed of their waste chemicals at these municipal dumps.

The Tijuana River

About 12 million gallons of raw sewage flow daily into the Tijuana River from the city of Tijuana. Health officials link incidences of hepatitis, vibrio cholera, amoebic dysentery, encephalitis, and two outbreaks of malaria to the sewage in the river. The Tijuana River is now unfit for any use. It is unsafe to go near the river in many places. Wildlife in most parts is either completely absent or seriously threatened. Beaches within several miles of where the river meets the Pacific Ocean have been closed for nearly 10 years.

At least three-fourths of the 530 Tijuana maquiladoras are in sectors of industry which generate hazardous wastes. They use heavy metals, organic solvents, caustics, and other toxic substances. Recent monitoring along the Tijuana River has confirmed the presence of heavy metals and industrial waste.

Sanford J. Lewis is director of Technical and Legal Support for the National Toxic Campaign Fund. Marco Kaltofen is Director of the Citizens' Environmental Laboratory, where Gregory Ormsby is a researcher. This was excerpted from their study Border Trouble: Rivers in Peril *published by the National Toxic Campaign Fund, Boston, MA, May 1991.*

The Environmental Effects of a NAFTA

David E. Ortman

A limited experiment with free trade is already underway between the US and Mexico, and the environmental effects are severe. The maquiladora 'Free Trade Zones' offer painful examples of the environmental problems of free trade.

Poor environmental controls have contaminated the drinking water of

US and Mexican citizens. In San Elizario, Texas, for example, a shared aquifer has been contaminated, and 35 percent of the children contract hepatitis A by age eight, while 90 percent of adults have it by age 35. Moreover, recent tests on both sides of the border at Nogales, Arizona indicate groundwater contaminated with pollutants released by the maquiladoras.

For the past two decades, over 95 percent of these industries could not account for their hazardous wastes as required by law, and few have implemented Spanish language programs to train employees about the risks of hazardous materials, according to the Border Ecology Project. The Project also found that, due to groundwater contamination by a common solvent used in these factories, the drinking water of Sonora residents is contaminated.

Excessive air pollution from the maquiladora industries is also well documented. The US National Park Service has stated that "emissions from industrial areas near Monterrey, Mexico significantly impact Big Bend and Guadeloupe Mountains National Parks, and extend as far north as Grand Canyon National Park, Arizona."

The European Community Experience

In November 1989, the European Commission published a study of the environmental effects of the implementation of the Common Internal Market in 1992. While the Europeans are undertaking a more ambitious project than the proposed North American Free Trade Agreement, their preliminary analysis is a confirmation of the environmental dangers of such agreements.

The task force explored a wide range of effects, the most significant of which was the increase in transportation that would result from greater trade. The task force concluded that the Common Internal Market would increase interstate truck transport in the European Community (EC) between 30 and 50 percent. According to the task force, "the growth impact of the Internal Market is likely to cause atmospheric emissions of SO_2 [Sulfur Dioxide] and NO_x [Nitrogen Oxides] to increase respectively by 8-9 percent and 12-14 percent by 2010."

While geographic differences between North America and Europe mean that these results cannot be translated directly, a dramatic expansion of truck traffic along the US-Mexican border seems inevitable. Some analysts even expect a doubling of that trade by the turn of the next century as a result of a North American Free Trade Agreement. The resulting pollution could be significant. The US Environmental Protection Agency has just taken a major step to try to improve visibility in the Grand Canyon. These measures may be overwhelmed by a hastily-concluded trade agreement. With the inclusion of Canada, one can reasonably expect growing transport across the US to Canadian markets as well.

The overall increase in transport would not only have effects on SO_2 and NO_x emissions but would also increase emissions of CO_2, the principal greenhouse gas.

The task force also points to some other dangers of trade and investment liberalization that North Americans would be well advised to consider carefully. In particular, the nations that are cobbling together a single Europe are at rather different levels of development – Germany being typical of the more developed 'North' of the EC, with Greece and Portugal being the less-developed 'South.' The task force is gravely concerned that investment in the South, both from private sources as well as official EC Structural Funds, will continue to be environmentally unsound. They conclude:

> Such investment can avoid severe negative environmental impacts if – and only if – an appropriate environmental management system is in place which guides investment to locations which can 'absorb' investment.

In North America the border areas of Mexico and the US are approaching – or have perhaps surpassed – their environmental absorptive capacity. An environmental management system will be a necessary part of a sound trade agreement, but without even a baseline impact assessment such a system cannot be crafted.

Finally, the task force points out that while the knitting together of the Single Market will force some member states to meet higher environmental standards, the incentive for trading partners outside the block, "will be to keep costs low and gain a competitive advantage by not investing in pollution control measures." Therefore, the report says, "Aid packages and trade agreements should envisage some minimal level of environmental protection in producer countries, and a programme of technology transfer will need to be implemented."

Two things are clear from Europe's experience. First, trade agreements and other market liberalization measures do have profound environmental effects. Second, these agreements must include environmental compensatory measures in order to avoid having trade be founded on competitive destruction of natural resources. In North America we believe that all three partner countries must take substantial national steps to avoid this unfortunate development. And, given Mexico's overall less-developed economy, we believe there will also have to be a substantial direct transfer of funds and technical assistance from Canada and the US to Mexico, so that the Mexican government does not exploit its environment or the health of its people.

David Ortman is the Northwest representative for Friends of the Earth. This was excerpted from congressional testimony he gave to the Subcommittee on Trade of the House Committee on Ways and Means, February 22, 1991.

Lax Enforcement of Environmental Laws in Mexico

Rodney E. Leonard and Eric Christensen

On paper Mexico's environmental law, the General Law on Ecological Balance and Environmental Protection,[1] is one of the more advanced among the developing countries. However, it is generally less restrictive than US law.[2] More importantly, the Mexican law has not been implemented. Mounting evidence demonstrates that Mexico's environmental laws are often not enforced.

For instance, the Mexican federal government budget for environmental law enforcement is only US$3.15 million.[3] Further, very limited human resources are available to the *Secretaría de Desarrollo Urbano y Ecología* (SEDUE), the Mexican environmental agency, for environmental law enforcement efforts.[4] SEDUE also lacks expertise to deal with complex environmental problems like hazardous waste.[5] Corruption is commonplace, and SEDUE officials frequently accept bribes from polluters.[6]

Similarly, the 1983 La Paz Agreement, in which SEDUE and the US Environmental Protection Agency pledged greater cooperation in enforcement of environmental laws, has been criticized for slow progress and lack of enforcement resources.[7] The American Medical Association's Council on Scientific Affairs has concluded that, "the present working relationship between the US and Mexico is not functioning well and cannot adequately cope with existing environmental conditions ... the prospects for success do not appear promising."[8] Cuauhtémoc Cárdenas, leader of Mexico's Party of the Democratic Revolution and a presidential candidate in 1988, states, "Most of the treaties and agreements Mexico and the US have signed in this field (environmental protection) are so far merely words on paper."[9]

Industry has been attracted to Mexico because of its lax environmental enforcement record.[10] Powerful incentives to move south are often created by the difference in environmental compliance costs between Mexico and the US. For instance, prices for hazardous waste disposal in the US range from $200 to over $2,000 per barrel, while disposal costs in Mexico are rarely higher than $200 and often considerably less.[11] Already, industries such as furniture manufacturing and metal-plating have fled to Mexico to avoid costly environmental controls.[12]

Professor Roberto Sanchez has attempted to quantify the number of industries that have fled the US for Mexico to escape stringent environmental regulations. His conclusions are startling. He found that:

> Ten percent of the maquiladoras in Mexicali considered environmental regulations to be among the main factors in the decision to leave the US, and 17 percent considered it a factor of importance. On the selection of Mexicali, almost 13 percent of the maquiladoras considered weaker environmental legislation in Mexico a main factor for relocation, and another 13 percent considered it a factor of importance.[13]

The flight of dirty industries to Mexico severely undercuts enforcement of US environmental laws. First, it defeats the purpose of those laws because pollutants still reach the biosphere and in many cases come back across the US border. Second, environmental regulators are stifled by industry threats to move to less restrictive jurisdictions.

Rodney E. Leonard, executive director of the Community Nutrition Institute, served as deputy director of the US Office of Consumer Affairs in the Carter Administration. Eric Christensen is a consulting attorney with the Institute. This is excerpted from their testimony before the International Trade Commission, April 12, 1991.

Footnotes

1. Published in the the *Diario Oficial de la Federación*, January 29, 1988, p. 23.
2. Cuauhtémoc Cárdenas, "Misunderstanding Mexico," *Foreign Policy*, Spring 1990, p. 123.
3. *Christian Science Monitor*, December 16, 1990, p. C5.
4. Roberto Sanchez, "Health and Environmental Risks of the Maquiladora in Mexico," *Natural Resources Journal*, 30: 163, pp. 178-179 and n. 32 (1990).
5. See Tomaso and Alm, *Economy vs. Ecology: Mexico's Drive for Growth Eclipses Concerns About Toxic Waste from Border Plants*, Transboundary Resources Report 4: 1 (Spring 1990); Roberto Sanchez, *Health and Environmental Risks of the Maquiladora in Mexicali*, Transboundary Resources Report 3: 1 (Winter 1989).
6. Cárdenas, *Foreign Policy*, Spring 1990, p. 123.
7. See eg, Sanchez, note 5; "Recent Developments – International Agreements – Agreement between the United States of America and the United Mexican States on Cooperation for the Protection and Improvement of the Environment in the Border Area," *Harvard International Law Journal*, 25: pp. 239, 244 (1984).

8. Council on Scientific Affairs, American Medical Association, "A Permanent US-Mexico Border Environmental Health Commission," *Journal of the AMA* 263: pp 3319, 3321 (1990).
9. Cárdenas, *Foreign Policy*, p. 123.
10. Cárdenas, *Foreign Policy*, pp. 122-123; Sandy Tolan, "Life in the Low-Wage Boomtowns of Mexico," *Utne Reader* (November/December 1990), pp. 46-47.
11. Sanchez, *Transboundary Resources Report*, note 5.
12. *New York Times*, March 31, 1991, p. 16; see also *The Journal of Commerce*, March 14, 1991.
13. Sanchez, *Natural Resources Journal*, 30: pp. 163, 185.

Agriculture

Free Trade vs. Sustainable Agriculture
Mark Ritchie

Two contrasting visions have emerged concerning the future of agriculture in North America. One approach, often referred to as sustainable agriculture, calls for social and economic regulations to protect the environment and family farms. This approach seeks to protect our soil, groundwater and fossil-fuel resources, and to promote economically viable rural communities.

Sustainable agriculture emphasizes the use of farming practices which are less chemical and energy-intensive, and it places priority on reducing the time and distance between production and consumption. This maximizes freshness, quality, and nutrition, while minimizing processing, packaging, transportation, and preservatives.

A competing vision, often referred to as the 'free market' or 'free trade' approach, pursues 'economic efficiency' aimed at delivering crops and livestock to agri-processing and industrial buyers at the lowest possible price, ignoring almost all social, environmental, health, and taxpayer costs. Based on traditional economic theories dating from the 17th and 18th centuries, this approach argues that any government intervention in the day to day activities of business diminishes 'economic efficiency.' Free-market and free-trade policies are heavily favored by the agribusiness corporations involved in the trading and processing of farm commodities.

Supporters of the free-market approach argue for the de-regulation of food production, under the rallying cry of 'getting the government out of agriculture.' They seek to scale back, eliminate, or de-couple farm programs such as price supports, supply management, and land-use regulations. In world trade, they support opening borders to unlimited imports and exports. Debate concerning the relative merits of these two views has become the central argument over modern agriculture policy. Agricultural trade negotiations under the auspices of the General Agreement on Tariffs and Trade (GATT) have pushed this controversy onto the front and editorial pages of the world's leading newspapers. President Bush's call for a Free Trade Agreement between the US, Mexico, and Canada will intensify this debate even further.

Agriculture and the Canada-US FTA

The US-Canada Free Trade Agreement was a serious setback for sustainable agriculture on both sides of the border. Canada, for example, had to weaken its stricter regulations on pesticides and food irradiation. And there was a concerted effort to get rid of supply management in the Canadian poultry, egg, and dairy industries. Both were seen as 'bad examples' by agribusiness, which feared that US consumers and farmers would begin to demand similar programs. The US-Canada deal, negotiated by right-wing governments in each country, shows that international agribusiness wins while family farmers, farmworkers, food-industry workers, and consumers tend to lose. The proposed continental free trade agreement will only heighten these inequitable gains and losses.

Agriculture and NAFTA

The principle threat to farmers in each country is wide-open borders. If governments cannot regulate the flow of goods coming into their countries, farmers, the environment, and national economies suffer devastating effects.

The US, for example, imposes strict controls on the level of beef imports, based on legislative authority in the Meat Import Act of 1979. Fast-food hamburger retailers have pushed hard to make sure that any new GATT or regional trade agreement will lift such controls, allowing the companies to import beef. Since beef can be produced more cheaply on cleared rainforest land in Central or South America, a sharp increase in US imports from this region, causing accelerated rainforest destruction, would almost certainly follow.

Unlimited beef imports would also obviously lower family income for US cattle producers. US producers would have to sell at lower prices to compete with rainforest beef, potentially the 'cheapest' (from a short-term perspective) in the world. They also would sell less, since much of the US supply would come from elsewhere. With more beef coming from overseas there would be a smaller market for US-grown hay, corn, and other foodstuffs. Replacing US beef with rainforest-fed beef thus not only devastates beef farmers in the US but also those who produce feedgrains.

FTA proponents claim that US grain farmers will increase shipments to Mexico under free trade. But the real impact is up for question. The Mexican government recently completed a barter deal with Argentina to bring over half a million tons of grain into Mexico, grain which could even be re-sold abroad if Mexico badly needed foreign exchange. Mexico, which is not even a major producer of grains, could actually end up as an exporter.

The implications of deregulated trade for environmental sustainability are staggering. Beef cattle again can serve as an illustration. Currently many US beef cattle are fed in huge, environmentally damaging feedlots. Many others, however, graze on the hillsides and meadows of the Upper Midwest. In Minnesota, for example, we have generally poor soil north of the Twin Cities, with the exception of the Red River Valley. It is hilly with thin topsoil and quite fragile. The only suitable agriculture for this land, and needed by this land, is cattle grazing, either for beef or dairy. As beef comes across borders and drives down the prices, Minnesota's diversified, small family beef operations will go under. The land will likely be put into row crops, soybeans or corn, to pay taxes and rent, soon depleting the thin soil. The political battle to encourage family farms and regulate factory-type feedlots would be blocked by free trade.

Eliminating Winter Produce in the US

US fruit and vegetable production also will be seriously threatened by free trade. US producers currently operate under substantial regulations concerning chemicals and workers. They pay higher taxes and extend more worker benefits than producers in most countries. Even if US and Mexican produce growers were regulated in the same fashion, however, the US Food and Drug Administration inspects only two percent of the food coming across the border. There is little chance that violators of food-safety regulations will be caught.

The entire US winter-produce industry could be threatened. If farmers in Florida, Texas, and California are to take the often enormous risks inherent in winter production they must be confident of steady markets, profitable enough to allow economic survival during years of complete crop losses. Unlimited imports would push weather and other risks to an unacceptably high level, eventually displacing US production. The consequent dependence on imported fruits and vegetables could have dire effects on US food safety and food security. And importing fruits and vegetables that can easily be grown in the US unnecessarily worsens the trade deficit.

Pillsbury Company's Green Giant division moved a frozen-food packing factory from Watsonville, California to Mexico in anticipation of a Free Trade Agreement which will allow them to bring products formerly produced in Watsonville across the border without tariffs and with few controls. Low wages and weaker environmental and safety regulations make the advantages obvious. Such agro-maquilas are the wave of the future should free trade advocates realize their dream.

According to Edward Angstead, president of the Growers and Shippers Association of Central California, total production costs for frozen broccoli in Mexico are less than pre-harvest costs in California. The biggest difference is the cost of labor. Angstead estimates the cost of farm labor in Mexico at $3 per day, compared with $5-15 per hour in California. The loss of Watsonville's Green Giant factory means that the farmers in the areas who grew crops for the plant lost a market. Farmworkers who picked those crops and the California cannery workers also lost jobs. The struggling community is already suffering.

NAFTA and Organic Farming

Free trade between the US and Mexico will deliver a 'double whammy' to farmers on both sides of the border trying to grow organic produce. The general lowering of prices on much commercial produce will make it harder to charge prices high enough to cover the organic producer's additional costs. Second, expansion of fruit and vegetable production in Mexico will increase the overall use of chemicals, further disrupting and interfering with natural pest-control patterns. Organic farmers cannot apply pesticides to control pests driven to their fields by neighbors' spray. They are dependent on proper predators for their own biological pest management.

Conclusion

A *real* trade and development agreement would address a wide range of trade-related issues for agriculture throughout North America. Export dumping, whereby subsidized US-based grain-trading corporations over supply the market and drive down market-prices in Mexico and Canada by selling grain at prices far below the cost of production, would be explicitly banned. Common food-safety regulations would strive for maximum protection of agricultural workers and consumers in all countries. Food security would be enhanced. The key question remains, "Can advocates for sustainable agriculture forge their own positive vision for a future set of economic, political and social relations among these nations?"

Mark Ritchie is executive director of the Institute for Agriculture and Trade Policy. This is excerpted from a paper of the same name he wrote for the Fair Trade Campaign, February 6, 1991.

Free Trade and Mexican Agriculture

Jorge Calderon Salazar

For several years Mexico has been undergoing a serious agricultural and food crisis, especially in the production of basic foods. This crisis is, to a large extent, due to the neo-liberal economic policies put in place by the past and present administrations. They substantially reduced public investment in rural development, deepened the decline in income and standard of living for rural inhabitants, and opened the country's border to the free import of agricultural products.

Crop prices have fallen significantly in real terms. Various government programs of technical and financial assistance to agricultural production have been dismantled. Credits from *Banrural* and other banks have undergone a sharp decline. The infrastructure for providing water and other services has seriously deteriorated as a result of almost a decade of governmental neglect.

Now the country is importing more than ten million tons of agricultural products. This means that a third of the population's food needs depends on foreign supplies. In addition to the serious effects for peasants and day laborers, this situation poses a threat to independence and sovereignty.

Most serious of all is that the government of Mexico is trying to deepen this agricultural dependence and to speed up the ruin of agriculture by signing a free trade agreement with the US and Canada. This agreement would make 2.7 million *ejidatarios*, small, cooperative farmers, who mostly produce basic foods, and a million small landholders, all of whom suffer grave problems of capital shortages, compete with the most advanced agricultural system in the world. US agriculture is dominated by monopolistic agribusiness firms who received over US$126 billion in subsidies between 1980 and 1987. These subsidies which the US government annually gives its farmers (US$26 billion in 1986 and US$12 billion in 1988) are between 10 and 20 times the total budget of the Mexican Ministry of Agriculture and Water Resources.

In the past eight years the per capita consumption of basic foods in Mexico has fallen by 30 percent as a result of the decline in real wages and the explosive growth in unemployment. This decline in purchasing power has kept average food imports at the already high level of ten million tons a year. Nevertheless it is necessary to point out that if the Mexican population had, on average, in 1990 consumed as much food as they did in 1982, the nation would have had to import half of its food requirements.

Faced with this serious agricultural crisis and the process of handing over natural resources and the best land to transnational corporations, which will speed up under a free trade agreement, it is necessary to defend the fundamental stipulations of Article 27 of the Mexican constitution. This article enshrines full national control over land, water and natural resources, and gives full legal rights and guarantees to *ejidos* and communities. It is necessary to fight energetically against the proposal for free trade and in favor of defending the country's agricultural sovereignty.

Jorge Calderon Salazar is an economist at the National Autonomous University of Mexico (UNAM) and director of ENLACE, a Mexican NGO for rural development. This was excerpted from a Common Frontiers Occasional Paper entitled A Free Trade Agreement and Mexican Agriculture *(Toronto, 1991).*

Human Rights

US-Mexico Free Trade Pact?
Not at the Expense of Human Rights
John Burstein

With keen interest in cinching a free trade deal, the Bush administration is loath to rock the boat by bringing up the delicate issue of human rights. Let's integrate trade now, they say, and worry about social issues such as human rights later. But it won't work, and every day it becomes more apparent that the two sorts of issues, being intertwined, must be treated together.

Human rights – including basic rights of physical integrity, political rights, and labor rights – are under growing assault in Mexico. Violations, as documented by both human rights organization and the 1990 State Department human rights report, range from torture in Mexican prisons to electoral fraud.

Amnesty International calculates that at least 80 percent of detainees are tortured, and there remain more than 500 unresolved cases of disappearances. Meanwhile, politically motivated violence has grown endemic. The center-left Party of the Democratic Revolution, created three years ago, claims more than 100 deaths and disappearances at the hands of government-linked forces. In the countryside, leaders of independent peasant organizations are targets of government-condoned violence and police harassment. Labor organizations defying the monolithic, is articlgovernment-linked Confederation of Mexican Workers are similarly under attack.

Freedom of the press? The London-based Article 19 human rights organization documents 51 killings of journalists between 1970-1988, and intimidation of the press has continued to the present.

Despite electoral reforms, the practice of fraud has been blatantly repeated in the states of Guerrero, Mexico, and Yucatan.

Despite legal reforms, including curtailed reliance on confessions and the passage of anti-torture laws, the implementor – that is, the court system – is still far from functioning adequately. Corruption and cronyism are central elements of that system – which has yet to prosecute a government official for human rights abuse. Indeed, a 'policy of impunity' reigns in Mexico, according to the most recent Americas Watch report.

Labor rights? The Confederation of Mexican Workers – whose members make up more than half of the country's organized labor – is thoroughly integrated with the governing Institutional Revolutionary Party (PRI), with attendant, significant restrictions on freedoms to associate, organize, and strike. Mexico's minimum wage is $3.50 a day in US money, and according to US State Department statistics, buying power has been halved in the last decade.

The fault for these abuses does not lie in Mexican law – Mexico's constitution is among the world's best for its protection of all manner of basic social and economic rights. The fault lies with implementation. Reform of these longstanding structures which have permitted or even promoted disregard for human rights is a massive political undertaking, even for the most well-intentioned leadership.

Is this the business of the US government? Mexico's human rights record is a highly appropriate concern of Washington in the context of our deepening bilateral relations. There already exists an array of US laws that conditions US foreign policy on respect for human rights generally. And, by the US International Financial Institutions Act, violations of internationally recognized labor rights constitute an unfair trading practice, a determination which prohibits special bilateral benefits.

And yet the Bush administration is intent on concluding the free trade agreement in the shortest time possible and on limiting the issues under discussion to tariffs, intellectual property, and investment.

Labor rights ought to be specifically included in the agreement. If not, labor exploitation in contravention of internationally recognized rights will continue and likely expand along with the expansion of foreign-owned industry. Similarly, acceptance of political and human rights monitoring and international dispute resolution mechanisms ought to be a condition of closer bilateral relations, to ensure stability and in accord with stated US policy goals of promoting respect for human rights and democracy.

John Burstein is a senior associate at the Center for International Policy. This is excerpted from his article in The Orlando Sentinel, *April 1, 1991.*

The Democratization Process in Mexico: A Human Rights Issue

Mariclare Acosta

Let me describe the current context of human rights in Mexico. We have what we call the traditional abuses – things like killings of peasant leaders over land conflicts. There is a very systematic pattern of killing *campesino* leaders in states such as Oaxaca, Guerrero, and Chiapas in the south. We also have many human rights violations that have to do with immigration and refugee issues because we are, as you know, a corridor for refugees fleeing Central America to the US. There are also very serious human rights abuses of indigenous populations over land use, ethnic rights, and language rights. And of course, we live with the legacy of the disappearances of the 1970s and the generalized corruption and abuses in the system of justice administration.

These traditional abuses still exist, but now, after two years of the Salinas administration, we have two recent trends that are very, very worrying. One of them is political violence. Members of the Partido de la Revolución Democrática (PRD) and PRD sympathizers continue to be killed. The PRD has just made a count and found close to 100 cases of killings of PRD sympathizers and activists. Some of the killings are related to electoral disputes, such as in Michoacan and Guerrero, where there were claims of electoral fraud during local elections and violence erupted as a result.

Another new manifestation of serious human rights abuses has to do with drug trafficking. The Salinas administration considers the enforcement of laws against drug traffic and drug abuse a national priority. In the first two years of his regime he created an anti-narcotics brigade in Mexico, under the administration of the Attorney General of the Republic. This anti-narcotics brigade committed very serious abuses. I won't go into all the horrifying cases, but I will mention one: nineteen women, young girls, were raped in Mexico City by the personal body guards of Coello Trejo, the ex-prosecutor of the anti-narcotics brigade.

Many of the major killings in Mexico are attributed to the brigade, which is also under a lot of pressure from the US government to enforce all the laws against drug-trafficking and to capture cocaine dealers and smugglers. So, the brigade is given free rein.

The US government held a congressional hearing on the situation in September 1990, and Americas Watch and Amnesty International testified that there was a human rights emergency in Mexico. At the same time, there has been a great mobilization of Mexican groups and political parties around this issue.

What has been the Mexican government's response? It's a two-pronged policy. On the one hand, the government has acknowledged that violations exist. Salinas first appointed a Director for Human Rights in the Ministry of the Interior. As a consequence, many political prisoners were liberated, there has been formal acknowledgement of disappearances, and the basic mechanisms for filing complaints have been put into place.

The creation of the ombudsman in the state of Aguascalientes was also important. But at the same time, the abuses persist. President Salinas, in his last State of the Union address, said that human rights are a major priority for his administration. In June, just four days before President Salinas was coming to Washington to meet with President Bush and talk about a possible free trade agreement with the US, the National Commission for Human Rights was created. The event was marked by a public celebration to which all the diplomatic corps was invited. Adolfo Aguilar Zinser, a political commentator in Mexico, remarked that this was the first time he knew of a government that actually celebrated the fact that it violates human rights.

Now this Commission does not really have any independence. The president of the Commission, Jorge Carpizo, is a very well-known lawyer, and said to be an honest man. He claims that the Commission functions as an ombudsman, but unfortunately, it does not. It has no prosecuting powers, and can only make recommendations. The Commission has a staff of 200 and they have received about 1,300 allegations of serious human rights abuses. They have taken up some cases and made 33 serious recommendations. However, three of these recommendations were turned down by the Attorney General of Mexico, who simply refuses to adopt them. So the Commission has run up against its first obstacle.

The Commission organized a 'Week against Torture,' and presented the government with twelve recommendations to modify criminal procedures.

These twelve reform measures will not necessarily put a stop to torture, but they will certainly make it more difficult. However, according to many legal experts, the measures do not go far enough. They take power away from judges and put it in the hands of the Attorney General, so it really only strengthens executive power. In any case, the President did announce these reforms, giving human rights priority, at least rhetorically.

But in actual fact, you have, for example, many allegations against Coello Trejo, the head of the anti-narcotics brigade. He was forced to resign, but was not prosecuted. He was named Consumer Rights Prosecutor (That created a stir among business people who said, "Now, we're going to get tortured if we raise prices!").

In terms of the free trade agreement, I think human rights is definitely on the agenda of negotiations, though I don't think either President Bush or President Salinas want it there. It was put on the agenda because of the concerns of the Organization of American States (OAS), Americas Watch, and public pressure. My view is that the National Human Rights Commission, which was hastily organized just before Salinas' trip to Washington, was an obvious attempt to show that Mexico was doing something about its human rights problem. Now, although neither president wants the issue addressed, some US Congresspeople do.

As a Mexican, I do not want the US government to monitor our performance in human rights, for many reasons. One of them is that the US has not ratified any human rights treaties; Mexico has.

I would accept international supervision by the UN or the OAS. Even though I do not want US Congresspeople to directly pressure Mexico, there are many things that can be done. Independent human rights organizations can put pressure on the US government to keep a watch on human rights abuses, and they can make sure the UN and the OAS keep pressure on Mexico because it is a signatory to both bodies. And finally, it is important for US activists to support the Mexican population and the 53 organizations in our Mexican human rights network that are out there fighting for human rights.

Human rights abuses in Mexico will not end unless we demand accountability from government officials for ordering and covering up crimes. The only way to enforce accountability is through real democracy, an independent Congress, an independent judiciary, and free elections. Until that happens, we will continue to have the situation described by Miguel Sarre, the ombudsman of Aguascalientes who resigned in November due to intense pressure from the government and because he worried for his life and that of his family. "When I was named ombudsman, " he said, "I had no credibility with the population, and the government was delighted. Now, we have the inverse situation. The population supports me completely, and the government won't have anything to do with me." This, I think, is the problem of human rights in Mexico.

Mariclare Acosta is president and co-founder of the Mexican Commission for the Defense and Promotion of Human Rights. This is excerpted from a talk she gave in Boston in November 1990, and printed in Resist Newsletter *(January 1991).*

Immigration

New World Border
Arnoldo Garcia

The demarcation at the US-Mexico border is more than a 2,000 mile jurisdictional line that cuts across North America. Once migrants cross this line northward, they risk becoming victims of a nakedly violent labor control. Countless migrants have nourished the US appetite for cheap labor with their blood.

The decision to leave one's intimate surroundings, to leave family, friends, familiar places, language, foods, customs, and traditions in order to find work in another country – is an anguished decision. To migrate is to be cut from one's roots and endure the tribulations of *homelandlessness*.

What happened to my own family mirrors current migrant experiences. My grandparents were internal migrants first, having to leave their home in southwest Mexico to find work during a severe economic depression at the turn of the century. Then, due to the turbulence of the 1910 Mexican Revolution, they ended up in northern Mexico. Once here, they crossed into the US in further search of survival and work. They worked throughout the Southwest as migrants before finally ending up in the Northwest, joining relatives who had gone before them. But the decision to leave Mexico was filled with bitterness. And it was also sustained with the hope of return, because no family or individual seeks to live on the road, to survive precariously from season to season, to work under intolerable conditions and to live in ramshackle camps.

For coming to the US, Mexican migrants are accused of drug-trafficking, terrorism, spreading disease, causing traffic jams, and pollution. And, they are being made to pay in blood for these charges:

- **March 1989:** Francisco Ruiz Chávez is shot twice (once in the back) by a Border Patrol agent after he attempts to defend his wife who was being beaten by the agent. She was seven months pregnant. Ruiz Chávez was charged with deadly assault, goes to trial and is found innocent of the charges. The agent is never charged.
- **September 1990:** Victor Mandujano, 17 years old, trying to escape back into Mexico, is chased and dragged off the international fence by a Border Patrol agent who kills Mandujano by shooting him point blank in the face.
- **November 1990:** Ernesto Zamores, 13 years old, is shot in the back by a Border Patrol agent using hollow-point bullets, as he is jumping back into Mexico at the international boundary fence between Calexico/Mexicali. Zamores suffers critical liver, stomach, and lung injuries as he falls on the Mexican side and is rushed off to the hospital by his buddies.

These are examples of the systematic violence Mexicans and those who look like Mexicans endure at the US border and elsewhere. And though the violence hits citizen, legal resident, and undocumented alike, the victims' common denominator is that they are Mexican. According to Immigration and Naturalization Service data, 45 percent of all undocumented workers in the US are Mexican. But over 90 percent of those arrested and deported are Mexicans.

San Diego is one of nine sectors along the US-Mexico border under intensive Border Patrol surveillance; it is considered the most violent area. The Border Patrol has 850 agents assigned to a 13 mile area between San Diego and Tijuana. Forty-five percent of all apprehensions of undocumented workers take place in this area. According to San Diego Sector Chief Gus de la Vina, 473,000 'illegal aliens' were deported in 1990 from this area alone.

Migrants in this sector are victims of the most virulent abuse and hate crimes perpetrated by the Border Patrol and racist groups. Muriel Watson, widow of a Border Patrol agent and founder of 'Light Up the Border,' where mainly white demonstrators park their cars at the border and aim their headlights into Mexico, stated, "We're not against the Mexican people. We need them to work in the fields. But we need some kind of program to bring them in."

The San Diego sector reported 195 violent encounters between October 1989 and September 1990. Over the last twelve months, at least 10 migrants have been critically wounded or killed by Border Patrol agents. No agent has ever been charged.

Human Rights Abuses

While the US government criticizes human rights abuses in Mexico, no such recognition is forthcoming about its own transgressions. But the Americas Watch *1990 Report* blasted the US government for abusing the rights of immigrants and refugees and criticized Border Patrol violence against Mexicans.

The American Friends Service Committee's Immigration Law Enforcement Monitoring Project (ILEMP) report, *Human Rights at the US Mexico Border*, covering May 1988 to May 1989, documented 814 victims of abuse at the hands of immigration law enforcement officials along the US southern border, including Florida. It declares that these cases are a *"minimum,* conservative" figure as many victims do not step forward or never know they have legal recourse.

María Jimenez, ILEMP director, said, "No one source can give you a definite accounting of shootings, other abuses, not even the government. And this points to a serious problem of accountability."

The New World Border

In the 1980s, sharp declines in living standards, increasing integration with the US economy, and the struggle for democratic change in Mexico have combined to give a new dimension to Mexican immigration into the US. The increased mechanization of agriculture, associated with US food companies setting up operations in Mexico, is displacing workers. In southern Mexico, the use of dangerous pesticides, many of them banned or severely restricted in the US, is causing environmental degradation and undermining the livelihood and health of indigenous farmworkers. All are forced to seek work elsewhere or, as a last recourse, to go to the US.

Victor Clark Alfaro, director of the *Centro Binacional de Derechos Humanos* (Binational Center for Human Rights) in Tijuana, said, "There are an undetermined number of Mexicans fleeing the country for political reasons. These ... add a new dimension to the phenomena of Mexican immigration. This is a flow of migration which for political reasons has remained invisible."

These changes – taking place against the backdrop of the FTA talks between the US, Mexico, and Canada – do not bode well for migrants at the border.

Arnoldo García is an editor of Crossroads *magazine and resource coordinator of the National Network for Immigrant and Refugee Rights. This is excerpted from his article in the May 1991 issue of* Crossroads.

Workers Are A Commodity, Too

Jorge Castañeda and Rafael Alarcon

There appears to be a growing awareness in the US that deterring undocumented Mexican immigration may be one of the less certain of the vaunted merits of a free trade agreement.

Labor mobility has been removed from the negotiating agenda by the Mexican side for one stated, largely fictitious reason – Mexico prefers to create jobs rather than export people; and one true but often silenced motivation – including immigration would significantly slow down the entire process.

There is growing acceptance that the 1986 Immigration Reform and Control Act has not brought about the sought-after reduction in undocumented immigration from Mexico. Apprehensions at the border – an imprecise measure of actual flows, but a good indicator of trends – rose sharply in 1990 and were close to the six-year record in the period ending in March. Several recent academic studies also found little evidence that the new law has been a deterrent.

The problem is that both the supply and demand sides of the immigration equation continue to favor greater flows, and the structures provided by the 1986 law are severely flawed.

On the demand side, deep structural changes in the US economy and urban population are generating a growing number of low-paying, unskilled jobs for Mexicans. Even in the current recession, there is increasing demand for labor-intensive services, more than for labor-intensive goods. Women, an important new factor in immigrant flows from Mexico, are often more able than men to find jobs in the expanding, and often informal, service sector – in restaurants, hotels, janitorial services, etc. Thus families are now accompanying heads-of-households who previously migrated alone; and these families are staying longer or settling down in the US as the seasonal nature of Mexican immigration gradually shifts to permanence.

On the supply side, the most important factor in generating migration continues to play its role: The wage differential between Mexico and the US remains extraordinarily high. According to *GEA*, a new analysis and consulting institute in Mexico that is finally providing the type of statistics that Mexico has traditionally lacked, more than 55 percent of wage-earning Mexicans make twice the minimum wage or less – about $7.50 per day, or under $1 per hour.

President Carlos Salinas de Gortari's entire economic strategy is based on attracting foreign investment through low wages to generate employment and distribute wealth through job-creation. This may happen in the long term, but for now the wage differential between Mexico and the US is wider than ever. It continues to make emigration to the US a highly attractive proposition for any Mexican, employed or not, be he or she a minimum-wage earner or a highly skilled professional. Furthermore, the new migration-generating regions of Mexico – Oaxaca, Guerrero, and Mexico City – are certainly not the areas that new foreign investment will flow to.

Indeed, the case can be made that mass immigration from Mexico to the US will continue to be a fixture of US-Mexican relations, regardless of immigration policy in the US and economic policy in Mexico. There are 'push' and 'pull' factors operating beyond the control of either: the aging of the US population and the growth of the Mexican population most likely to emigrate; the shift from manufacturing to a service economy in the US; the 'reception committee' syndrome, whereby existing communities of immigrants are a strong enticement for newcomers – this to be strengthened by the long-term effects of the 1986 law, as Mexicans with legalized status go on to naturalization and eligibility for family reunification.

The choice for the US, then, is not between undocumented immigrants and none at all, but between legal flows and illegal ones. The free trade negotiations could be just the time for a new realism to replace the illusion that undocumented immigration can be staunched.

A free trade agreement should include emigrant workers, not to slow them down, or to shoot it down, but because it is in the interests of both countries to do so, and because the time is right for doing so.

Even American labor, which has been adamantly opposed to any kind of immigration reform tending toward legalization, might dwell on the demographics of undocumented Mexican immigration and the consequences in a state like California: more workers without rights or unions, without protection, without a stake in the system, without a voice in government, without security, but still coming to the US in large numbers, independently of policies or attempts at restriction. Is gradual, negotiated and selective legalization truly more detrimental to US society than unstoppable, undocumented migration? The existence of a large, unprotected, over-exploited foreign, illegal underclass is bad for any society; it is particularly pernicious for one that has become as much of a two-tier society as has the US.

Free trade can become another immigration-deterring pipe dream like the Immigration Reform and Control Act, or a propitious occasion for resolving this most delicate and substantive of bilateral issues.

Jorge G. Castañeda is a Professor of International Studies at the National Autonomous University of Mexico (UNAM). Rafael Alarcon is a doctoral student at the University of California, Berkeley. This is excerpted from their article in the Los Angeles Times, April 22, 1991.

3. Alternatives

ON YOUR MARKS -- All set for the fast track?

From *The Other Side of Mexico* No. 20 March-April 1991

Introduction

John Gershman
The North American Free Trade Agreement (NAFTA) offers both challenges *and* opportunities to citizens' movements and grassroots organizations across North America. It has provided a crucial opportunity to re-examine the relationships between the three countries of North America. The NAFTA offers an ambitious, compelling vision – a flawed vision, as the previous section illustrated – but a vision nonetheless, of an economically integrated North America. But while there are a multitude of criticisms one can bring to bear on this vision, their impact will be limited unless they are linked to an equally ambitious and more compelling alternative vision for a North America facing the 21st century.

If the NAFTA has sparked a long-overdue re-examination of the relationships between Canada, the US, and Mexico, it has also served as a catalyst for wider debates. It has challenged citizens' and grassroots movements to question the conventional wisdom of economic development in general, as well as traditional methods and strategies of defining and organizing to advance local and national interests.

Continental Visions

Cuauhtémoc Cárdenas, Sandra Sorensen, and the Mobilization on Development, Trade, Labor, and the Environment present, respectively, Mexican, Canadian, and US perspectives on alternative visions of an economically integrated North America. They emphasize some common themes, such as the democratic participation by citizens in shaping the decisions that affect their lives, and understanding trade, investment, and other economic issues as tools to attain broader objectives – justice, equality, sustainable development – rather than as ends in themselves.

The presence of common threads does not preclude the existence of differences, reflecting the range of perspectives and concerns of the citizens of these countries. Rather than claiming a false unanimity in the face of the challenges posed by the NAFTA, these alternatives reflect the diversity of the alternatives to continental development by corporate design, and highlight broader questions about the meaning of development itself.

The Broader Development Debate

The free-market policies pushed by the Bush Administration and its allies in Latin America have contributed to making the 1980s a lost decade for the overwhelming majority of Latin Americans, Asians, and Africans. Both economic inequality and environmental destruction have accelerated as the poor majorities of these countries pay the price for the excesses of their ruling elites, the profit margins of commercial banks, and the onerous conditions of World Bank and IMF structural adjustment policies.

Robin Broad, John Cavanagh, and Walden Bello show that the grassroots movements that emerged in response to the failures of technocratic development strategies offer a different vision of development grounded in a set of principles: participation, sustainability, and equity. Sprouting up in the margins of economies ravaged by cuts in government spending, debt servicing, and structural adjustment programs, these grassroots organizations ask, 'Development for whom?'

David Morris analyzes the ideology of the 'global village' that underpins the 'growth at all costs' strategy, and offers an alternative vision of a 'globe of villages,' rooted in economic exchange that enhances communities' capacity for self-sufficiency and self-reliance.

John Gaventa, Barbara Smith, and Alex Willingham discuss grassroots organizations in the southern US who are asking "Development by whom? Toward what end?" raising fundamental questions about not only who controls and benefits from economic change, but what role economic growth plays in a vision of development that also includes democracy and human dignity. Linking these concerns requires movements to adopt new methods of organizing and to develop new ways of linking local issues to global changes.

New Strategies

As Primitivo Rodríguez points out, one of the risks of organizing around the NAFTA is that people will orient strategies toward short-term goals, such as democratizing the negotiating process, or integrating a social charter with a FTA. But if the NAFTA represents a dramatic restructuring of the world economy, heralding the new world order of global production in a post-Cold War era, then such limited approaches will ultimately fail. The strategic vision for confronting the NAFTA challenge must be long-term and comprehensive not because of idealism or rhetoric, but for reasons of realism and relevance.

The new terrain of the world economy has forced trade unions, among other groups, to re-think their methods and goals in organizing. Rachael

Kamel discusses the experience of one of these new organizations, *La Mujer Obrera* (The Women Worker). Based in El Paso, Texas, La Mujer Obrera is a predominantly Chicana movement of textile and garment workers that is also working with workers in the maquiladoras in Juarez on the other side of the Rio Grande.

La Mujer Obrera and groups like it demonstrate that organizing in local communities must transcend the traditional dichotomy of workplace or community issues to encompass the range of social relationships that shape people's everyday lives. These relationships require addressing issues of race, culture, and gender as well as the more 'traditional' concerns of economic development. Increasingly, these relationships have an international dimension.

That dimension is the subject of Jeremy Brecher and Tim Costello's contribution, which identifies important initiatives, such as the Coalition for Justice in the Maquiladoras, and the Fair Trade Campaign, which are already engaged in transnational organizing, linking local and global realities in creative and effective ways.

The challenges and opportunities posed by the NAFTA – of alternative continental visions, the meaning of economic development, and the need for new methods of organizing are addressed here. But the final judgement as to the success or failure in meeting these challenges will be determined in neighborhoods, factories, fields, and communities across North America – by the success or failure of grassroots movements to develop visions, strategies, movements, and policies that can confront the corporate juggernaut and translate hopes, dreams, and visions into reality.

Continental Alternatives

The Continental Development and Trade Initiative

Cuauhtémoc Cárdenas

We face a challenge no other generation of Americans, Mexicans, and Canadians have encountered: to prepare for the future by creating a framework of genuine continental cooperation. If we succeed and establish a mechanism for sharing fairly our respective talents and resources, our economies will be strengthened and our people will live better, not at the expense of the wealth of the neighbor but thanks to each other's prosperity. However, we must not be misguided by false illusions or self-indulgence; such compatible and equitable prosperity will not come automatically.

To have a new relationship, to do things the right way, Mexicans and Americans, in particular, must acknowledge that the existing premises of our economic integration are not necessarily adequate to build a just and viable new relationship. The exploitation of cheap labor, energy and raw materials, technology dependency, and lax environmental protection, should not be the premises upon which Mexico establishes links with the US, Canada, and the world economy.

We cannot be satisfied with the kind of future that would emerge from a simple economic liberalization. This would extrapolate present trends and exacerbate present vices. Instead, we should act with vision, to see and meet the future, not simply wait for it. Let us be responsible and prudent: not any kind of trade is a mutually advantageous exchange, not any type of investment is going to transform our productive foundations and create the jobs and incomes we want for our people; not any kind of industry is going to optimize the use of our resources and protect our habitat; not any profitable business is a responsible enterprise. Economic liberalization is not our objective, it is one of our tools. Development, social justice, and a clean environment are our objectives.

We are in favor of a broad Continental Trade and Development Pact that primarily includes free trade between Mexico, the US, and Canada and that is, at the same time, in the interest of Mexico's development and not at the expense of US or Canadian welfare standards.

We know that there are those who consider that any agreement is better than no agreement; that for Mexico any access to the US market is a sufficient basis for accepting indiscriminate American demands, since that access is both a necessary and sufficient condition for Mexican development. We reject that stance. Trade, we insist, must be an instrument of development, not an end in itself.

The Continental Trade and Development pact we propose offers an opportunity to engage in a new North-South dialogue, no longer with the sole purpose of drafting declarations, but to sign economic pacts and share actual development commitments. What we want to create is not defensive blocs or exclusive clubs but a new system of cooperation and integration between developed and developing countries.

If Mexico, the US, and Canada are capable of molding their respective development objectives in an unprecedented understanding, this consensus should be the core of a new alternative process of multilateral negotiations for hemispheric integration. The Caribbean and Central America could join first, followed by the Andean and southern cone nations of South America.

We propose an ambitious negotiation for a coherent, integrated, global approach conducive to a broad, long-term continental free trade and development pact. The proposed FTA currently on the table, while nowhere near as broad ranging as the one we propose, is certainly not a strict trade deal. It includes the American trade-linked agenda – investment, services, intellectual property, and energy – but nothing from the Mexican trade-linked agenda – compensatory financing, labor mobility, environment, and a social charter.

The alternative agreement we propose consists of five clearly defined negotiating baskets: First, strictly trade related matters; second, adoption and harmonization of norms in the following areas: investment, anti-trust regulations, a social charter, the environment, and intellectual property; third, compensatory financing; fourth, dispute settlement mechanisms; and fifth, labor mobility. Let me outline briefly the content of these five negotiating tracks.

Trade

The guiding criteria to bring about free trade must be that reciprocity is not yet applicable except under very specific, exceptional circumstances. American and Canadian access to Mexican markets in those areas still protected must be gradual, selective, and cushioned with adequate additional resources. On strict trade matters, this agreement must be above all an agreement that removes or reduces US non-tariff barriers.

As a general development strategy, Mexico's aim should be to change the entire maquiladora scheme as a first and very important step. After more than 25 years of operation the maquiladora's backward linkages remain virtually non-existent. The maquiladoras have created nearly half a million jobs in 25 years and generate some support for the balance of payments. However, a large number of them cause serious environmental damage and nowhere is the gap between productivity growth and wages as dramatic, nor have real wages remained so low for as long a period of time compared to any other sector. This proves that under this type of arrangement, neither Mexican wages nor living conditions can be expected to rise significantly.

Subsistence agriculture, which produces most of Mexico's basic grains, must be removed from the bargaining table. Millions of peasants will be thrown off the land if their inefficient, backward, and uncompetitive forms of production are suddenly exposed to the volatile world commodities market. The modernization of Mexican agriculture will not be achieved by following a path that any successful industrial country would reject for themselves. We need a radically new agricultural policy, one which goes beyond mere trade liberalization.

Norms

Investment: We must learn to see foreign investment not as an unavoidable evil, but as a desirable opportunity and even a necessary instrument to attract resources, to close technological gaps, and to move decisively into world markets. The partnership we want will not be created if we do not redefine the rules governing foreign investments in Mexico. Such broad redefinition should emerge from a frank, truly open, and plural national debate.

Those sections of the laws and regulations limiting foreign investment in Mexico that we believe must be maintained have to do with access to natural resources and the strategic sectors of the economy, mainly oil. The existing state monopoly on the exploration, extraction, refining, and industrial transformation of Mexico's oil must remain intact and be excluded from any negotiation. This obviously includes, from our point of view, any commitment to a guaranteed supply of oil to the US, in contrast to what Canada accepted in the US-Canada Free Trade Agreement. On the issue of oil, Mexico's negotiating position should be inflexible; any deviation from this norm is unacceptable and could lead to deep political divisions. The oil industry is to Mexico what the military and the aerospace industry is to the US – a question of national security.

Social Charter: The existing disparities among the three economies imply that a substantive, central objective of these negotiations should be the gradual but decisive standardization of trade-related norms. First and fore-most among these must be a social charter, ensuring that workers in the three countries enjoy the same real – not merely on paper – work-site conditions, collective bargaining rights, legal framework, and occupational safety and health standards in order to avoid the exploitation of Mexicans and present unfair competition to their American and Canadian counterparts. Wages cannot be decreed into uniformity, but the conditions under which they are established, and the framework in which labor and management relations take place, can be harmonized.

The Environment: The harmonization of norms should also be implemented with respect to the environment. The agreement should set limits to each other's access to natural resources. Mexico cannot become a chemical waste or garbage dump for American or Canadian industries trying to get around environmental restrictions in their countries. Laxity in the enforcement of environmental laws in Mexico must cease to be an advantage for companies investing in Mexico. One of the main contributions of a continental pact to international cooperation would be the agreement among parties that the responsibilities and costs of protecting the environment are to be considered development costs and investments.

It is also necessary to harmonize consumer protection norms; it is unacceptable that products, substances, and procedures deemed dangerous, unfit, or toxic in the industrialized nations should be considered fit for the underdeveloped ones.

Environmental norm harmonization does not mean the immediate adoption of exactly the same norms by the three countries but rather their fastest possible evolution in the same direction.

Compensatory Financing

The disparities between the three economies mean that, over and above the market-induced funds that could come as a consequence of the FTA, Mexico will require substantial funding to finance, first, the adjustment process, including needed investments in infrastructure and education in order to absorb additional new investments; second, the harmonization of norms and third, the provisions of a social charter.

We know that financing is not easy, but making the fundamental disparity of the three economies the cornerstone of the agreement means making compensatory financing its centerpiece.

Settlement of Disputes

With regard to directly trade-related disputes, the mechanism that is set up, in addition to or in substitution of the General Agreement on Tariffs and

Trade (GATT) mechanism, must include provisions which parties from the three countries can resort to in equal terms. The way to achieve it is simply by extending the authority of a trade-related tripartite dispute settlement mechanism. Concurrently, provisions must be adopted to allow mechanisms of social verification of compliance, such as equal access to the dispute settling mechanisms for all concerned parties: manufacturers, growers, unions, environmental associations, consumer groups, human rights associations, etc.

Labor Mobility

A genuine economic negotiation between Mexico and the US could not conceivably avoid the controversial issue of labor mobility across the border. This is the most significant economic, social, and human exchange between our two countries, and thus sufficient reason to have migration at the top of our agenda.

We understand the difficulties and recognize that there are deep cultural sensitivities and even racial resistance toward Mexican and Latin American immigration.

Ideally, Mexicans should not have to leave their country to find jobs in the US. Creating economic opportunities for all is no doubt our greatest aspiration. A free trade agreement is seen by many on both sides of the border as a bold economic move needed to stem immigration flows at their source by creating jobs for Mexicans in Mexico. Furthermore, some believe that an FTA with no social conditions attached to it will create the best of all possible worlds for US industry: direct access to a permanent pool of cheap labor on the other side of the border. However, free trade alone might very well give impetus to the migration process instead of killing it.

It is understandable that many Americans do not want an open border with Mexico. It is equally comprehensible that Mexicans wish to do away with the humiliating and often repressive controls and limitations on border crossings. The very reason for negotiating on this issue is to find an intermediate, common ground between open borders and undocumented immigration beneficial for both parties. Legal and broad access for Mexican labor to the US job market that protects the rights of Mexicans in the US, in realistic and socially acceptable terms both from an American and from a Mexican standpoint, is surely possible.

A shortsighted, narrow, trade agreement will only bring prosperity for the few and a loss of hope for the many. A trade liberalization conceived and conducted within the framework of a real development alternative will mobilize the enthusiasm and commitment of many social groups in Mexico who today see themselves excluded from every benefit. We have the obligation to succeed with this opportunity to bring true progress and fruitful cooperation between our nations.

Cuahutémoc Cárdenas is the leader of the Partido Revolucionario Democrática (PRD) and was a presidential candidate in the 1988 Mexican elections. This was excerpted from a speech he gave in New York on February 4, 1991.

Developing Healthy Economies
An interview with Sandra Sorensen
What's your alternative to continental free trade – or global free trade for that matter?

What we want is healthy economies. We have to talk about the economy in terms of people. A simple way to describe a healthy economy is that in a healthy economy, the people are healthy. They have food to eat and clothes to wear, they have a place to live, their environment isn't toxic, they are physically safe, and they get adequate health care. On top of that I would add that their mental health is taken care of: they have enough access to education and leisure time to appreciate their family, their friends, their culture, the natural environment. They feel like they're making a meaningful contribution to society.

I'm not talking about everybody being rich. I just mean everybody should be able to live with dignity.

How would you start building healthy economies?

In terms of Canada, rejecting free trade would mean returning to a greater level of self-reliance. If you base your whole economy on the world economy – over which you have no control whatsoever – it's a bit like going out every day and betting the farm on a poker or a crap game.

So you're promoting a kind of protectionism?

I'm promoting economic self-reliance. Self-reliance means we have to decide what industries are necessary to Canada's well-being and then make sure they survive. For instance, some people argue that the Canadian dairy industry is not economically viable – that it's not 'competitive' – so therefore we should get rid of supply management for the dairy industry and let Americans truck in dairy products from hundreds of miles away.

It's true that Canadian dairy products are very often more expensive than American ones, for some very good reasons: heating costs are higher here, and people tend to get better wages in the Canadian industry than they would in the US. As a result, milk and milk products are more expensive.

But it's not as if dairy farmers are putting millions in Swiss bank accounts. The money they earn goes almost entirely to employing local people, buying local inputs for their farm operations, and buying consumer goods locally. That money gets used over and over by their community and actually provides the money consumers use to buy the milk. That's the thing about a sustainable economy – money goes around.

Now, if you all of a sudden drive those dairy farmers out of business and bring in milk and cheese from the US, a lot of business activity in Canada dries up. Canadian communities suffer. Money is going out, but it's not coming back in.

The Americans know all about this. They have launched more protectionist trade actions in the last decade than any other country. They've got too much money flowing out, and they're trying to get some to flow back in.

I'm promoting a sort of 'global public health' model where the economic environment is healthy, and countries can interact without fear of being slaughtered by economic diseases like free trade.

In Canada, what kind of program would you put in place to replace free trade?

It would look at strengthening the economy from the bottom up, not from the top down, the latter is the basic idea behind free trade and 'trickle-down' theories of economics. The first priority is economic development, not trade. Trade can be a useful tool of economic development, but as we've seen with the Canada-US FTA, more trade doesn't necessarily bring economic well-being.

Now, when I say 'development' I'm not talking about pouring out tons of government money to build a bunch of industrial parks in Saskatchewan or Labrador in the hope that this will be enough of an incentive for private investors to set up operations there. An example of where that has worked is in Mexico's maquiladoras. But really the maquilas 'work' because labor costs are kept at next to nothing. That kind of slavery is the ultimate subsidy to business. That's not what we want for Canada or for Mexico. I'm talking about development that uses a country's resources to ensure people's basic needs and quality of life.

In Canada, we have an embarrassment of riches in terms of natural resources. But we've got to stop wasting them and giving them away. The Alberta government's sale of one-third of the province to Japanese and American pulp companies is the kind of thing that just can't happen. Alberta taxpayers get something like $1.40 in tree royalties for every ton of paper produced. But a ton of paper is worth anywhere between $1,300 and $2,000. All that money is pouring out of the country and we're losing our forests. It would make a lot of sense to cut down fewer trees and employ more Canadians on the processing side. That's where the money is. This concept of being only 'hewers of wood and drawers of water' is not the answer.

Some industries that we'll want to keep might have to be restructured for environmental reasons. I'm thinking of the pulp and paper industry in particular. The technology already exists for them to stop putting toxins into the water system. We have to require that.

One thing that's sucking wealth out of Canada is that so many Canadian companies are being sold to foreign companies since free trade went through. When that happens, all the profits that used to stay in Canada go to the US or to France or wherever. There is no guarantee that any of those profits will be re-invested in Canada. We have to start assessing foreign investments on the basis of whether they are actually new investment for production in our country or whether it's just a buyout of the kind which will cost us jobs and currency.

In terms of industry, we need flexible policies that are tailored to individual industries. As I said, I look at it first of all in terms of deciding which industries we as a country feel are essential. For the ones we need to defend, there are all sorts of tools available: import restrictions, export taxes, tariffs, content requirements, rules requiring governments to buy Canadian, that sort of thing.

All of these suggestions I'm making would give Canadians more democratic control over their resources. We also need stronger democratic economic institutions that give people more control over their work. This means more co-operatives, a certain number of publicly-owned corporations, a healthy small business sector, and strong unions. I suppose in principle we could talk about democratizing the multinational corporations that are responsible for the abuses of democracy that we're fighting against.

I don't think Canadians realize just how much free trade has undermined our democracy.

What do you mean?

Well, ask yourself this: if they had had a choice, would British Columbian fish plant workers allow Canadian fish to be processed in the US? Would workers in furniture plants, glass plants, or auto parts plants send their jobs to the US voluntarily?

Obviously not. In Canada under free trade, corporations – mostly from the US – decide who will lose their jobs, who will lose their business, who will have to take a pay cut, and who will be poor. The role of government is to stay out of the way. If people get hurt, too bad. That's what Mulroney calls 'modernizing' the economy.

I like the framework put forward by Carlos Heredia, who is a leader of the Mexican Action Network on Free Trade. I think it's significant that his number one priority is democracy. Now, they have really basic democratic needs in Mexico. They need to be able to reorganize unions. They need honest elections.

But we need to reform democracy in Canada, too. 'One person, one vote' is supposed to mean everyone has the same say in how we run the country. But this isn't true in Canada today. I think most Canadians realize that a single mother living on welfare in Regina or St. John's does not have the same political influence as the Chief Executive Officer of a big corporation. I mean, technically speaking, their votes are worth the same, but the single mother has not been able to spend money promoting parties or candidates who will speak on her behalf in government.

Even though we have a certain level of political democracy, it's obvious that we don't really have political equality because of economic factors.

But what does this have to do with free trade?

One very high-profile example was in the 1988 election, where we saw business groups set a new record for election spending. When they thought their free trade project was in danger, they went hog-wild spending money on advertising. The Canadian Alliance for Trade and Job Opportunities spent something like six million dollars promoting free trade. And that's not counting money spent by different corporations and different corporate bodies like the Business Council on National Issues.

Would you say business is over-represented in government?

To be more specific, the main group that's over-represented in Parliament is well-to-do white men. Within this group, a lot of them come from business backgrounds, so it's natural for them to think in terms of what's good for business. They tend to think, "Well, what's good for business is good for the country" – mostly because what's good for business has always been good for them.

But what's best for big corporations is very seldom what's best for the majority. It's one of the reasons we have so many poor people in our rich country. It's one of the reasons acid rain keeps falling.

Sandra Sorensen is the Executive Director of the Canadian Centre for Policy Alternatives. This interview was excerpted from the Pro-Canada Dossier *#29 (January/ February 1991).*

Expand the Agenda
Mobilization on Development, Trade, Labor, and the Environment

The statements of the Bush, Salinas, and Mulroney Administrations on a proposed North American Free Trade Agreement are extremely narrow in scope, focusing primarily on trade and investment. Inasmuch as the growing integration between our countries involves massive flows of debt payments and immigrants, and affects labor, environment, human rights, and development, we demand that these issues be part of any tri-national negotiations.

Development

As Mexico, Canada, and the United States are currently at different levels of development, any agreement must take these differences into account. It must also consider that, to varying degrees, development in each of the three nations has been pursued in ways that have been detrimental to women, children, indigenous populations, people of color, and the poor. The people of each country must maintain the right to determine their own social, economic, and environmental priorities subject to the regional goal of improving conditions in each of these areas. Trade and investment should not be seen as ends in themselves, but as tools toward development, social justice, and a healthy environment.

We agree that trade should support a process of development that is based on the principles of enhanced national and local self-reliance in key sectors, increased economic equity among citizens of each country, environmental and economic sustainability, and the broadest possible popular participation in national decision-making.

In accordance with these principles, the people of each nation have the right to protect local efforts at achieving viable rural communities, sustainable and subsistence agriculture, and food self-reliance and food security for all citizens. We also recognize that indigenous peoples in all three countries may have different development aims and that any agreement between the three nations should respect their right to manage their own resources sustainably and to shape their economic destinies.

Increased trade and economic relations between the three nations have the effect of narrowing the gap in the labor, environmental, and other conditions of the three countries. Further economic integration that is not conditioned on basic worker and environmental standards will continue to narrow the gap in the direction of lower conditions. Any agreement should be conditioned on deliberate steps by all three countries to pursue a higher-wage, higher-skill development path.

Human Rights

Human rights — including basic rights of physical integrity, political rights, labor, and other economic rights — are under growing assault in Mexico. Abuse of the human rights of immigrant, indigenous, and other communities in the US and Canada also continues.

Acceptance of political and human rights monitoring and international dispute resolution mechanisms ought to be a condition of closer relations between our nations. As our governments pursue closer economic relations, they should reaffirm their commitment to the principles and procedures of previously-signed international agreements, including the Universal Declaration of Human Rights, the American Declaration of the Rights and Duties of Man, the Charter of the Organization of American States, and the American Convention on Human Rights.

Debt

The US and Mexico rank first and third in the world in terms of total debt owed to foreign sources. In both cases, service payments on the debt have been eating up growing shares of government expenditures and hence have been diverting resources from pressing domestic problems. Canada's external debt, while smaller than that of the US, is greater on a per capita basis, and puts heavy upward pressure on interest rates. Debt-reduction schemes must be a central component of any tri-national initiative if any meaningful and sustained development is to occur.

Trade and Investment

Increased trade and foreign investment can be a positive force, but it must be carried out in a fashion that serves the development needs of the three countries. In each country, large numbers of people feel that it is in the national interest to preserve and strengthen domestic production capacity in certain sectors and control over certain natural resources.

The specific roles that trade and foreign investment should play in each society should be subject to open and pluralistic debate. And, further, liberalization of trade and investment should not occur without binding and enforceable standards that protect workers, communities, and the environment in all three countries.

Labor

In recent years, the opening of trade among the United States, Canada, and Mexico has been accompanied by a fall in wages, benefits, and working conditions. True economic development cannot be achieved by worsening the already excessive maldistribution of income and wealth or limiting the ability of workers to participate fully in economic and social life.

Any agreement between the three nations should also be based on recognition and respect for the systematically violated human and labor rights of immigrants and refugees, documented and undocumented. In addition, guest worker programs between the US and Mexico, which have fostered exploitative working conditions both for migrant and US workers, should be addressed in any comprehensive agreement.

Environment

Comprehensive development and trade agreements must incorporate effective environmental regulation. Otherwise, increased trade can fuel unsustainable and environmentally damaging industrialization, as the experience with Mexico's maquiladora industry demonstrates.

A preliminary list of requirements that should accompany any comprehensive development and trade initiative includes the following:

- assessment and public disclosure of potential environmental risks from proposed actions and alternative actions related to the agreement,
- development of waste, sewer, water and air pollution prevention infrastructure, particularly in the environmentally-stressed border area between Mexico and the US,
- safe management and disposal of hazardous materials and disclosure of hazards in the workplace,
- elimination of international trade in domestically prohibited pesticides and other products,
- measures and assistance to ensure effective enforcement of environmental standards in each country,
- revocation of trade advantages for corporations that do not comply with basic environmental standards.

Binding Enforcement Mechanisms

Any comprehensive agreement among the US, Mexico, and Canada, must include a formal and binding dispute resolution mechanism that links compliance with fundamental labor and environmental rights and standards to the economic concessions granted under the agreement. The dispute resolution body should be empowered to withhold trade and other concessions from governments and corporations to the extent that those governments and corporations gain a competitive advantage by their failure to observe environmental and labor standards.

Dispute resolution proceedings must be open to the public. All panel decisions, including interim decisions, should be made public and should be published in a form accessible to a wide range of citizens. In addition, a mechanism should be included in the dispute resolution structure allowing interested members of the public to bring complaints against either governments participating in the agreement or corporations benefitting from it. Any enforcement mechanism would operate as a supplement to, not a replacement of, national environmental and labor laws, judicial and administrative procedures and enforcement mechanisms.

In addition, the US Congress should enact legislation requiring all corporations registered in the US to observe US environmental and labor standards, or their equivalents, when operating overseas.

The Mobilization on Development, Trade, Labor and the Environment (MODTLE) is a coalition of over 60 organizations that is based in Washington, DC. This is excerpted from a statement issued on May 1, 1991.

The Broader Debate

US Plan for Latin Debt Relief Is a Non-Starter

Robin Broad, John Cavanagh, and Walden Bello

The lessons of the 1980s teach that there are no shortcuts to development. Development strategies will not succeed and endure unless they incorporate ecological sustainability, equity and participation, as well as effectiveness in raising living standards.

Out of the generalized failure of development over the 1980s, there is a different kind of consensus emerging among people the Western development establishment rarely contacts and whose voices are seldom heard. A new wave of democratic movements across Latin America, Asia, and Africa is demanding another kind of development. In citizens' organizations, millions of workers, farmers, women, and environmentalists are saying they want to define and control their own futures.

Alan Durning of the Worldwatch Institute estimates that across the developing world, more than 100 million people belong to as many as several hundreds of thousands of these organizations. Many are informal economic institutions that have sprung up to fill the economic void left by cuts in government spending. There are examples of successful worker-owned businesses, transportation collectives, peasant leagues, micro-enterprise credit associations, and other citizens' initiatives across Latin America that are touching larger and larger numbers of people.

These movements reject the heavy emphasis of free-market development on exports based on cheap Latin American resources and labor. For the southern half of our hemisphere, the only possibility of creating a market of consumers possessing effective demand is to eliminate the severe inequalities that depress the purchasing power of workers and peasants. The 'how-to' lists here all require government action, through such steps as land reform and advancement of worker rights.

Building development dreams on cotton, timber, minerals, and other ecologically damaging exports is not only unsustainable, it fails to ask the more fundamental questions of whom the development should benefit. Instead, building an export base on top of a strong internal market makes sense. In this scheme, foreign-exchange receipts would shift from primary commodities to processed commodities, manufactures, and environmentally sensitive tourism.

Why should citizens' movements pushing for a more equitable, sustainable, and participatory development stand a chance in the 1990s? Most of the answer lies in the extraordinary possibilities of the current moment.

For four decades, the Cold War has steered almost all development discussions toward ideological arguments over capitalism versus socialism, markets versus governments. It has also diverted public attention away from non-ideological global concerns (such as environment, health, and economic decay) and toward the Soviet Union as the source of problems.

The dramatic winding down of the Cold War should, at a minimum, open real debate about development that gets beyond sharply drawn ideological categories. What are the proper roles of government and market? If one values both effectiveness and equity, what kinds of checks should be placed on the market?

Citizens' movements have played a central role in the transformation of Eastern Europe. A greater opening should emerge from this phenomenon. Governments and development experts should treat such non-government organizations with the respect they deserve.

Instead of a free-trade initiative, Latin America desperately needs substantial debt relief that would provide the resources for sustainable development. But debt relief is not enough. If there is ever to be a more unified and sound Western Hemispheric market, the marginalized millions of the hemisphere must be made effective consumers and, more importantly, central participants in planning their future. Indeed, these are the people with whom George Bush should discuss future initiatives for the hemisphere.

Robin Broad is an assistant professor at American University in Washington, DC. John Cavanagh is a fellow at the Institute for Policy Studies. Walden Bello is executive director of the Institute for Food and Development Policy.

A Globe of Villages

David Morris

Let me now explore the possibilities and strategies for a new kind of world economy, one whose metaphor would be a globe of villages, not a global village. This would be a planetary economy that emphasizes community and self-reliance. Such self-reliance would not be the same as self-sufficiency. As biologist Russell Anderson suggests, self-reliance is "the capacity for self-sufficiency, not self-sufficiency itself." It gives us the capacity to survive if cut off from suppliers by natural or man-made intervention. It encourages us to maintain a diversity of skills within our societies and to localize and regionalize productive assets. It is a strategy that welcomes 'foreign' capital, but not at the expense of local ownership; that promotes competition but also encourages cooperation; and that recognizes the value of the voluntary sector as a vital underpinning of civil society. It is a strategy that emphasizes prevention rather than treatment and that looks towards a society which promotes satisfaction rather than consumption.

Once dismissed as 'Utopian', the paradigm of a globe of villages is already beginning to help solve pressing national and local problems. Take that of waste. In the US, pressure from local communities has led to the closure of many existing domestic waste dumps and a refusal to build new ones, with the result that the costs of waste disposal have rocketed over the past decade, rising faster and further than the cost of oil in the 1970s. Although rising disposal costs spawned many innovative techniques and technologies to solve the domestic waste problem, local and national officials continued to approach the problem with the analytical tools of the planetary economy. Defining waste as a disposal issue rather than as an economic development opportunity, they opted for the solution that demanded the least institutional or political change: incineration.

In doing so, they not only voted to continue – and perhaps even expand – the consumption of raw materials, but they also chose a 'solution' that itself generates considerable quantities of waste for disposal – namely, a toxic incinerator. Inevitably, the dumping of toxic ash has led to considerable local opposition, thus perpetuating the waste crisis.

Now consider an approach to waste that embraces the paradigm of a globe of villages – one that attempts to strengthen community by reducing imports and capturing the maximum value from local resources. One that emphasizes resource efficiency while also trying to maintain and expand the productive capacity of the community.

Take the example of scrap tires, a small but troublesome waste item. Every American throws away the equivalent of one 20 pound tire a year, causing numerous environmental problems. Many tires resurface years after they have been thrown away. Tire dumps have caught on fire and burned for months. And the stagnant water in tires provides an ideal breeding ground for mosquitos. As a result of all these factors, Minnesota banned land disposal of tires two years ago.

Tires can be shredded and burned but that captures only the direct energy value, maybe a penny a pound at today's oil prices. Tires shredded into even finer pieces can be added to road asphalt and be sold for a few pennies more. But the real benefit comes when the scrap is concerted into a valuable final product. A Minneapolis-based firm developed a liquid polymer that can be added to pulverized tires which allows the scrap tire to compete both with virgin rubber and with plastics. Its product, TireCycle, sold for about 50 cents a pound. For Minneapolis and St. Paul, the cost of tire disposal in 1985 was about $4 million. If all tires could be recovered, treated and sold for 50 cents a pound, the Twin Cities would avoid almost all of their disposal costs, in addition to creating a new industry with $20 million in gross sales.

But the opportunity was lost: as part of a well-intentioned but poorly-designed rural development scheme, the Governor of Minnesota used state financial subsidies to lure the new Tire-Cycle plant to northern Minnesota, and thus away from its source of supply, the Twin Cities. As a result, the tires for recycling had to be transported 200 miles north to the plant, and the final product had to be shipped an equal distance to its nearest markets. The plant went bankrupt in early 1990.

Time for a Change

The challenge then is to move away from the paradigm of the planetary economy and to create in its place an economy that allows us to produce most of what we need from our own local human, natural, and capital resources on a sustainable basis. In that respect, I agree with John Maynard Keynes when he wrote:

I sympathize with those who would minimize, rather than with those who would maximize economic entanglement among nations. Ideas, knowledge, science, hospitality, travel – these are the things which should of their nature be international. But let goods be homespun whenever it is reasonably and conveniently possible and, above all, let finance be primarily national.

Goods should be homespun to maintain a productive capacity and the skills associated with producers. When we abandon our ability to produce for ourselves, when we separate authority from responsibility, when those affected by our decisions are not those who make the decisions, when the cost and the benefit of doing things are not part of the same equation, when price and cost are no longer in harmony, we jeopardize both our security and our future.

We also undermine democracy. Thomas Jefferson warned us that democracy depends on the widespread distribution of property. By property, he meant the ownership of productive assets. In his time, the ideal democrat was the yeoman farmer, the multi-skilled and largely self-reliant man and woman. Having the capacity to be self-reliant, such a person would be less willing to sell a vote for hand-outs from a political party. Having the knowledge of how things are made, and how the natural world works, such a person would be an informed participant in the political process.

One may argue that free trade is not the cause of all our ills. Agreed. But free trade as it is preached today nurtures and reinforces many of our worse problems. It is an ideological package that promotes ruinous policies. And most tragically, as we move further down the road to giantism, and planetism and dependence, we make it harder and harder to take another path. If we lose our skills, our productive base, our culture, our traditions, our natural resources, if we erode the bonds of personal and familiar responsibility, it becomes ever-more difficult to re-create community.

Which means we must act now. We need to challenge the postulates of free trade head on, to preach a different philosophy, to embrace a different strategy. There is another way, but to make it the dominant way we must change the rules, indeed, we must change our own behavior. And to do that requires us not only to challenge the emptiness of free trade but to promote an economics as if community matters.

David Morris is co-director of the Washington, DC-based Institute for Local Self-Reliance. This article was excerpted from The Ecologist, *Volume 20, No. 5 (September/October 1990).*

Development, Democracy, and Dignity

John Gaventa, Barbara Ellen Smith, and Alex Willingham

There is a new level of participation by grassroots citizens on matters of the economy. The new participation transcends class, racial, gender, and community lines. It is characterized not only by demands for a fair share of the economic pie, but also by demands for redefining the very basis of economic priorities and economic decision making. Indeed, the failure of the dominant economic policies to provide for fair and equitable economic change presents the economy as 'contestable terrain,' a legitimate arena for grassroots action and dissent.

The strategies for the new participation are also highly diverse. They vary, in part, according to the economic context in which grassroots groups find themselves and range from alternative development, to fighting to save traditional jobs and communities, to organizing and empowering the new.

With the failure of the traditional model of development from without, many local groups have turned to creating their own alternative development from within. The strategy of creating alternative development builds on local skills and resources. Though not limited to them, this strategy seems strongest among communities and groups who traditionally have been excluded from the formal economy. In the process of creating alternatives to traditional development, they create new models of local control, self-reliance, and participation.[1]

Other groups work to develop strategies that challenge the control and responsibility of those who have defined the traditional development policies in the region. Struggles to fight plant closings and protect workers' rights in existing industries are important, for they challenge the accountability of capital to community and insist that the rights of workers and communities are more important than a blind belief in maintaining a favorable climate for business. These battles against deindustrialization by default are often taking place in communities whose histories have been shaped by earlier processes of industrialization by a formal economy, and they involve coal miners, textile workers, other workers, and their unions.

The current strategies and constituencies involved in workplace organizing around new jobs may be quite different from those involved in workplace organizing in the past. Today they are often led by new entrants to the work force, especially women and people of color, and they link community and workplace issues.

The struggles for alternative development, for protecting old jobs and communities, and for organizing the new are at one level diverse and separate. But at another level, the efforts are interconnected; they all speak to the common concern of creating spaces in which grassroots communities participate in defining their own economic futures. The questions, they suggest, are not only about substituting one set of policies for another. Rather, they are about who shall participate in shaping the policies in the first place, and how success will be defined. They ask not only 'Development for whose interests?' but also, 'Development by whom? Toward what end?' They reflect demands not only for economic development but also for economic democracy, not only for growth but also for quality of life and dignity.

The process of broadening the definition of who participates in the development debate leads, of course, to different definitions of what constitutes success. As strategies to take charge rebuild the link between 'community' and 'economy,' it becomes artificial to separate the economy as a single issue from other concerns. At the local level, 'the economy' is part of a broad web of relationships which includes the relationship not only to a job or employer but also to the land and environment. Economic concerns become more holistic, more than just a paycheck. They also involve personal relationships to family, community, and culture.

Within that web, just as demands for development cannot be separated from demands for participation, neither can they be separated from concerns of dignity and equity, be they based on class, race, or gender. The mutual struggles for development and for dignity mean crossing barriers that traditionally have divided social groups.

Newly formed efforts are bringing together unions, civil rights organizations, and community groups to link their common concerns. In November 1987, more than 5,000 people marched in Nashville as part of the 'Jobs with Justice' campaign, one of the largest demonstrations in the region since the civil rights movement. Later coal miners and other union members joined the leaders of the Southern Christian Leadership Conference for a symbolic march across the South, representing a new unity across race and region that was not present twenty years ago.

At the same time, there is much to be done if these local efforts are to translate themselves into a movement. More steps and strategies are needed to link and expand the emerging community-based activity.

First, this new participation in the economy implies the need for economic education. Education, in this sense, is not for the purpose of adapting to new jobs in an economic model over which people have no control, but it is for helping people recognize the validity of their own knowledge of their economy and begin to create new definitions of development that would be successful in their terms. It is a process of gaining the economic literacy needed to act and participate in economic decision-making and economic change.

Second, the movement for economic justice must begin to translate its increased awareness and activism about economic matters into a new, more democratic economic policy. In many ways the failure of the traditional state and local economic policies based on the industrial recruitment model – low wages and corporate tax breaks to create a 'good business climate' – has created a policy vacuum which is ripe for new ideas that could be supported by diverse and broad constituencies. Federal legislative and policy interventions were crucial to the growth of the civil rights movement in the South. In the same way, the movement around economic issues must involve governmental participation if local action is to be sustained. And, given trends in the federal government that favor devolving many policies for economic well-being back to the states, the local level takes on new significance as a building block for policy change.

While emphasizing local grassroots action, we argue at the same time that the regional economic crisis is part and parcel of a national and international crisis as well. Just as constituencies and issues must be linked within the region, so, too, must locally-based movements make links with those concerned about change in the larger arena. To do so involves building horizontal links with other regions and groups in the country whose own futures are being played off against our own. We must recognize that while important gains have been made in our region, they have often been achieved with the help of broader structures – progressive churches, unions, foundations, some government agencies – which now often battle for their own survival at the national level. We must also tie local efforts to national ones, remembering that the linkage needs to be a two-way process, one that mandates national groups to hear and include the voice of the grassroots, and the grassroots to join movements for a more progressive agenda nationally.

Finally, the nature of the current crisis challenges us to link local and international concerns. Often, in our movements for social change, domestic concerns have been seen as separate from international issues. The movement of capital and industries from home to abroad and the playing off of workers and communities across national boundaries link local and international concerns in a new way. In recent years, many groups in the region have begun to respond to the new conditions by developing their own grassroots exchanges with groups affected by similar issues elsewhere. For example, the Africa Peace Tour sponsored in 1987 by church and community groups linked economic and political concerns in southern Africa to those in the Deep South. A tour of health and safety activists from India following the Bhopal disaster linked groups questioning the location of hazardous industries, which occurs in poor communities here as well as abroad.[2] Similar exchanges have brought together leaders of cooperatives in Nicaragua and Alabama, and of rank-and-file democratic unions in Mexico and Tennessee.

While national and international restructuring serves on the one hand to deepen inequities in the South and to challenge traditional models of economic development and social change, so, too, has it spawned the seeds of a new movement. At the moment, the movement is at the grassroots, relatively invisible to the national eye. To grow, it will need broader economic education, coalition building, policy development, and national and international linkages. But as the new participation builds, it has the possibility of transforming contemporary economic restructuring into a new model of development, one that links matters of the economy to matters of democracy and dignity – at the local level as well as in the broader arena.

John Gaventa is the director of the Highlander Research and Education Center. Barbara Ellen Smith is the author of numerous articles on labor and women's issues in the South. Alex Willingham is a professor of political science at Williams College, Williams, Massachusetts, and has written on voting rights and black political participation. This was excerpted from their chapter in Communities in Economic Crisis: Applachia and the South *(Philadelphia: Temple University Press, 1990).*

Footnotes

1 For other accounts of grassroots development activity, see *Everybody's Business: A People's Guide to Economic Development,* a special edition of *Southern Exposure* 14, nos. 5-6 (September/October and November/December 1986).

2 See, for example, Anil Agarwal, Juliet Merrifield, and Rajesh Tandon, *No Place to Run: Local Realities and Global Issues of the Bhopal Disaster* (New Market, Tenn.: Highlander Research and Education Center, 1985).

Action

Mexico is 'In' Again

Primitivo Rodríguez

The Bush-Salinas proposal of June, 1990 to initiate free trade negotiations has turned Mexico from a 'distant neighbor' into a close partner. This time around though, the US-Mexico relationship has two special characteristics:

- Key social groups such as trade unionists, environmentalists, immigrant rights advocates, and Latinos are prepared to play a crucial role to affect the outcome of the free trade negotiations.
- The negotiations serve as a catalyst to review the overall Mexico-US relationship and its impact on the Western Hemisphere.

In principle these two elements look very promising, both in terms of opening the bilateral relationship to sectors previously uninterested in it or ignored in its development, as well as in building a strategy to advance shared perspectives among the peoples of the Americas. The path in these directions, though, will require important changes in the way social groups have traditionally looked at and organized for advancing their own and their nations' interests.

The signing of a free trade agreement will have a dramatic impact on the way Mexico and the US perceive and deal with each other. Failure to sign it, however, won't erase the increasing integration, economic and otherwise, between the two neighbors. In either case, the bottom line is clear: Mexico and the US cannot plan a better future for themselves without building a fairer and more productive relationship between them.

The reality of growing US-Mexico integration is what moved the Salinas and Bush administrations to seek a better-planned and mutually beneficial relationship through a free trade agreement. That same reality can also provide the basis for a strategic and long-term relationship between, let's say, environmentalists and labor and human rights advocates on both sides of the border.

Bi-national cooperation between these and other interested groups cannot be only for tactical and, therefore, short-term purposes, such as opening the free trade negotiations to Congressional debate or modifying a free trade agreement. Rather, on the occasion of the debate surrounding the FTA, the opportunity exists to develop a vision and an agenda to respond, from a peoples' perspective, to the challenges presented by transnational production zones, a global economy, and a post-Cold War era. To do so is not a matter of solidarity or idealism, but simply of realism: to change or to become irrelevant.

In this context, the re-discovery of common ground between US and Mexican social groups leads necessarily to a transnational vision of our shared concerns and interests. In fact, as a response to the internationalization of production and capital investment, some social groups from the US and Mexico have already started a promising interchange that will hopefully lead to the dismantling of barriers imposed by narrow and fragmented interests based on nationalistic perspectives that are increasingly ineffective in enhancing rights and a better life.

We will have to move beyond the narrow agenda of the FTA to include broader issues. For instance, efforts directed to introduce labor and human rights issues into the FTA, or in parallel legislation, must address the full inclusion of labor and human rights for undocumented immigrants. The criminalization of the right to work for undocumented immigrants has not only led to abuse and discrimination, but also to undermining cooperation between Mexicans and North Americans, as well as labor rights and trade unions' organizing potential.

Even before Canada became a participant in the free trade negotiations, contacts had been opened among Canadian, US, and Mexican social groups. In so doing, the prospect of a 'North American Common Market' seems to be reinforced. However, President Bush recently introduced the 'Enterprise for the Americas Initiative,' proposing a free trade zone from Alaska to Tierra del Fuego. For its part, the Mexican government has stated that in seeking an FTA with the US, Mexico wants to serve as a bridge to the rest of Latin America.

Taking all this into account, Canadian, US, and Mexican social groups will need to join efforts with their counterparts from the rest of the Americas. Fortunately, international networks of trade unionists, native peoples, women, environmentalists, and human and immigrant rights advocates already exist to take on this task.

Primitivo Rodríguez is the director of the Mexico-US Border Program of the American Friends Service Committee. This is excerpted from an AFSC mailing dated January 2 1991.

The View from El Paso

Rachael Kamel

For those who live and work at the border, the maquila economy is an ever-present reality. And unionists in border towns like El Paso are among the most active in cross-border organizing. To call attention to maquila issues, the El Paso Central Labor Council – a local grouping of AFL-CIO affiliates – has sponsored demonstrations blocking the bridge to Juarez. In July 1988, El Paso unionists brought thousands of pounds of food to donate to striking workers in Juarez.

More recently, the El Paso union council held a press conference inside Juarez to express their support for an independent union there. The closeness of the two communities – as well as the family, cultural, and language ties between El Paso's many Chicano workers and their Mexican neighbors – has made cross-border communication easy and informal.

This ease of communication makes El Paso one of the few US communities where cross-border interaction also reaches non-unionized workers. "We've learned a lot from groups on the Mexican side," comments Cecilia Rodriguez, "including many of our most valuable lessons." Rodriguez is director of *La Mujer Obrera* (The Woman Worker), an El Paso center for garment and textile workers, 85 percent of whom are women, mostly Chicanas.

It is not too many years since El Paso, with its thickly clustered garment plants, was known as the 'Jeans Capital of the World.' Then, in 1985 and 1986, more than 13,000 workers were laid off. Many of the plants moved just across the border to Juarez. Today, says Rodriguez, some jobs are returning – but "the new jobs offer no benefits, no guarantees to the workers. Employment in the industry is still very unstable.

"Given the economic situation in the textile industry," Rodriguez continues, "the unions don't know what to do. They are at a loss. We feel that we have to develop new strategies – and also challenge the unions to respond better to the needs of unorganized workers."

One approach taken by La Mujer Obrera is organizing workers' committees inside the textile plants. "The first goal for these committees," says Rodriguez, "is to pressure the companies to publish personnel policies. The way things work now in the sweatshops is that the owners have total control – they do what they want, when they want. We have a suit pending in the Texas Supreme Court, in which we argue that personnel policies should have contractual force." The suit stems from a 1985 case in which CMT Industries, a local garment manufacturer, promised its work force a paid holiday for Labor Day and then reneged after the workers had already taken the day off.

Already, the factory committees have won several rulings from the Texas Employment Commission and the National Labor Relations Board. Union affiliation may be an option for the long term, says Rodriguez, "but in our present situation, it's just not realistic."

Work inside the plants is complemented by a strong emphasis on leadership training and organizational development. "The economic devastation of our communities cannot be described," says Rodriguez. "It is like living after a war. To survive as a community, we need people with certain skills – organizing, or technical skills like translating or grant-writing. It is very hard to find people who can do these things but who also respect textile workers and believe that they are human beings. If we can train the workers themselves in these skills, three-quarters of our battle is won."

A Women-of Color Network

This emphasis on organizational development has prompted La Mujer Obrera to form a network with other women-of-color organizations in Texas, New Mexico, and California. "For women of color," says Rodriguez, "these questions are not being addressed on a national level, and we cannot tackle them by ourselves on a local level. We need to understand what is going on with multinational corporations and what strategies will allow us to deal with them."

To sustain itself over the long haul, Rodriguez believes that groups like La Mujer Obrera also need to attend to their own economic base. "The future for groups like ours is not very bright," she comments. "Funding is drying up. Our newest campaign is to start some small economic projects that could provide a permanent income base for us."

In all of these approaches, La Mujer Obrera has been heavily influenced by its connections with Mexican women's groups. Notes Rodriguez: "We've learned from working with them the importance of building in leadership, a political analysis, and a long-term perspective when you're trying to build an organization. We've begun to integrate more economic analysis into our work. We've learned to use a popular education approach," that teaches skills for critical thinking based on people's own life experiences.

"When you're dealing with multinational corporations," Rodriguez concludes, "you can't be complacent. It's a big help to us to be on the border. Our situation is difficult, politically and economically, but we have the advantage of being exposed to a model of organizing that comes from a Third World country."

In some ways, however, La Mujer Obrera is the exception that proves the rule. A majority of US workers touched by the global factory are not reached by unions. This is especially true for women workers. When they organize, it is more likely to be through small, community-based groups than through traditional trade unions.

Such grassroots organizations often develop the most creative strategies for meeting the needs of unorganized workers. They are also far more likely to appreciate the problems women face in combining family and workplace responsibilities. Because they lack an institutional base, however, they tend to be poor in resources, and they seldom have access to international channels of communication.

The same problem exists on the Mexican side of the border. Cecilia Rodriguez and many other women trade unionists say that the Mexican groups they feel closest to are informal bodies that operate outside any institutional structures. They too are bypassed by formal trade-union channels, and they too lack resources of their own for international networking.

The problem is redoubled for grassroots groups in other Third World countries, which are farther from the US than Mexico is both in distance and in culture. Thus, for groups that seek to organize around the global factory, a central challenge is how grassroots groups and unorganized workers can be included in any international dialogue.

Rachael Kamel is a journalist. This was excerpted from her book, The Global Factory: Analysis and Action for a New Economic Era *(Philadelphia: American Friends Service Committee, 1990).*

Global Village vs. Global Pillage: A One-World Strategy for Labor

Jeremy Brecher and Tim Costello

It was once a crime to organize a union or call a strike in the US and most other countries. Trade unionists were regularly fired, blacklisted, beaten, arrested, and sometimes murdered. Establishing the rights to assemble, organize, bargain collectively, strike, and participate in the political process was the focus of a century of struggle.

Workers in much of the world are today struggling to establish these same rights. An international labor rights movement has developed to support them. Like Amnesty International and other well-known human rights organizations, it publicizes abuses and mobilizes support for the victims. Beyond that, it aims to incorporate labor rights requirements in national and international trade, investment, and lending policies.

In the US, the first target for the international labor rights movements was the Generalized System of Preferences (GSP), a program designed to help developing countries by letting them bring products into the US duty-free. Noting that GSP was encouraging countries like Korea and Taiwan to produce goods for the US market under tyrannical conditions, labor rights advocates in 1984 persuaded Congress to declare a country ineligible for GSP if it "has not taken or is not taking steps to afford internationally-recognized worker rights." The rights specified were:

- the right of association,
- the right to organize and bargain collectively,
- a prohibition on the use of any form of forced or compulsory labor,
- a minimum age for the employment of children,
- acceptable conditions of work with respect for minimum wages, hours of work, and occupational safety and health.

Labor rights advocates in the US, now organized as the International Labor Rights Education and Research Fund (ILRERF), won another victory when Congress, in the 1988 Trade Act, defined the denial of internationally-recognized labor rights as an 'unfair and unreasonable trade practice' against which unilateral action could be taken under international trade rules.

Not surprisingly, the Reagan and Bush Administrations have done little to apply the labor rights provisions of US trade law. Indeed, they have turned the law to their own political purposes, applying the GSP restrictions to such countries as Nicaragua and Romania, while refusing even to hold hearings on such blatant violators (but US 'friends') as El Salvador, Guatemala, Indonesia, the Philippines, and Turkey.

Nonetheless, experience so far indicates that the law could have a potent effect. In 1988, for example, AFL-CIO and human rights groups, working closely with unions in Malaysia, submitted a petition charging that industry-wide unions were outlawed in the electronics industry there. When the US Trade Representative (USTR) stated it would accept the petition for review, the Malaysian government announced that such unions would be permitted in the electronics sector. Within a few days organizing efforts were underway in the electronics plants. But when the USTR ruled Malaysia was "taking steps" to afford worker rights and therefore qualified for GSP, a relieved Malaysian government, under strong pressure from the electronics industry, restored the union ban.

In 1990, the ILRERF launched a campaign to incorporate labor rights provisions in the General Agreement on Tariffs and Trade (GATT). Under Congressional pressure and with growing support from European governments, the USTR proposed that GATT establish a working party on labor rights.

No labor rights working group was established before GATT negotiations collapsed in December, 1990. Now, Pharis Harvey, executive director of ILRERF, notes, "With the rapid shift toward regional trading pacts, it's not clear if GATT will even survive. But all the members of the Organization for Economic Cooperation and Development (OECD – an organization of the most industrialized nations) voted for a working party on labor rights. So the next focus is likely to be inclusion of labor rights provisions in the OECD and/or regional trade agreements."

The Maquiladora Coalition

In February 1991, a group of US and Mexican organizations announced the formation of the Coalition for Justice in the Maquiladoras, whose goal will be, in effect, to harmonize upward the standards for maquiladora workers and their communities. Their statement of mission declares,

> We are a binational coalition of religious, environmental, labor, Latino, and women's organizations that seek to pressure US transnational corporations to adopt socially responsible practices within the maquiladora industry, that will ensure a safe environment on both sides of the border, safe work conditions inside the maquila plants, and a fair standard of living for the industry's workers.

The Coalition has developed a "Maquiladora Standards of Conduct" to provide "a code through which we demand that corporations alleviate critical problems created by the industry." Its 22 provisions address a wide-range of the abuses with which the maquiladoras have been charged.

The code incorporates many labor and environmental standards already required by Mexican law, but poorly enforced in the maquiladoras. According to Betty Baumann, former Maquila project director for the American Friends Service Committee, "Mexican labor law is probably the most progressive in the whole world, but nobody pays any attention to it."

The tentative strategy for the Maquiladora Coalition is to select in each part of the border region one target company where organizing efforts are already underway. On the US side, stockholder meetings and resolutions will be used to publicize abuses and to demand corporate responsibility. Supporters on the Mexican side will organize the public and members of the Mexican Congress to press for the enforcement of Mexican law. The campaign will not attack the maquiladoras themselves, which have support from the government-affiliated Mexican labor federation, but rather will emphasize the need to enforce reasonable standards.

Fair Trade Campaign

While the recent GATT negotiations were trumpeted as the way to establish a 'free trade' regime that would benefit the entire world, environment, labor, farm, and other people's organizations in both the Third and the First World looked at them with great suspicion, seeing them as an effort by transnational corporations to break down all regulations that might resist their depredations.

In the US, a Fair Trade Campaign initiated by family farm groups brought together a coalition of environmental, consumer, farm, and some labor organizations to challenge the US GATT proposals. It has focussed on mobilizing grassroots political pressure to improve or block the proposed agreement.

While the US government has been promoting its free trade proposals as beneficial for both US and Third World agriculture, many critics argue that it primarily benefits agribusiness and transnational commodity traders – and would drive millions of small farmers in both North and South off their farms. Farmers have been organizing internationally since the early 1980s. Says Mark Ritchie of the Fair Trade Campaign,

> We learned to reverse the old slogan, 'Think globally, act locally.' We learned you have to act globally to succeed locally – you have to go to Brussels to save your farm in Texas. It was really important for farmers in different parts of the world to see their common circumstances and to develop win/win approaches, rather than being played off against each other.

The Mexican FTA

A transnational critique of the Bush FTA plan is already underway. Thirty-six US congressmen led by Rep. Don Pease wrote President Bush that "the real challenge before trade policy-makers in the US and Mexico is to find ways in which to guide and manage growing US-Mexican trade ties in mutually beneficial, equitable, and human terms."

The Congressmen pointed out that "neither the US government nor the Mexican Government has recognized publicly the need to incorporate a social charter in a US-Mexico FTA to address fundamental labor, health, environmental, and political policy differences that exist between the two countries." They noted the salience of Mexico's "authoritarian, undemocratic, one-party system," the government's domination of the Mexican labor movement, the wage gap, the weakness of Mexican environmental and public health standards, and the issues of drugs and immigration.

A response by six leading Mexican scholars, writers, and diplomats endorsed the need for any agreement to include a social charter. They added that an agreement should protect the human rights of Mexicans in the US and preserve Mexico's control over its oil resources. And they argued that low Mexican wages should not be the basis for economic integration. Such a basis would be "too humiliating and unproductive for Mexican dignity and economic development, too costly in jobs and welfare for American and Canadian workers, and too destructive for our common environment and civilization."

US-Mexican economic integration may have the potential to mobilize a significant response at the grassroots. When a Minneapolis business consultant held a breakfast seminar in October to promote the benefits of maquiladoras for Minnesota companies, 50 people from unions, women's groups, and community action programs rallied and chanted outside their meeting room with the message, "The maquiladora system means exploitation of Mexican workers, exploitation of the environment, and the loss of jobs to communities in the US." (The consultants eventually called the police to break up the rally.)

Unions in the Twin Cities organized a conference on 'Solidarity vs. Competition in an Era of Free Trade,' to which they invited labor, environmental, and other representatives from Mexico and Canada. Similar efforts elsewhere could rapidly generate a continent-wide movement.

Jeremy Brecher is a community-based historian and Tim Costello is a truck driver and workplace activist teaching at the University of Massachusetts, Boston. This was excerpted from their Global Village vs. Global Pillage: A One-World Strategy for Labor *(Washington, DC: ILRERF, 1991).*

4. Resources for Action

The ideological embrace of free markets and free trade in the last decade has led to a confusion of means and ends. Free markets are not ends in themselves. If they are a means to decentralization of power within society, and thus democracy, and if they set in place economic incentives that deliver broad-based prosperity, then they deserve our support. But to the extent that they subvert our moral values and economic interests, they must be rejected or modified. We agree with what President Franklin D. Roosevelt said in 1937 with regard to the US Fair Labor Standards Act, i.e. that "goods produced under conditions which do not meet rudimentary standards of decency should be regarded as contraband and ought not be allowed to pollute the channels of ... trade."

Pharis Harvey, executive director of the
International Labor Rights Education and Research Fund,
in testimony before the US Congress, 1991.

Introduction

John Gershman

Compelling visions, like those described in the previous section, are not enough. What can we do to make them a reality?

In the short period of time that groups working on North American free trade have joined forces, they have created a true debate in the national press, forced the Bush Administration to address some new issues, and have sparked the formation of new citizen alliances.

The struggles of organizations like *La Mujer Obrera* are forging bonds of solidarity between workers on both sides of the border that are linking economic issues to a range of other issues that shape their everyday lives. National networks like the Mobilization on Development, Trade, Labor, and the Environment in the US, Action-Canada, and the Mexican Action Network on Free Trade are forging national and tri-national linkages, to construct a vision of an economically integrated North America based on dialogue, equity, and social justice.

The struggle to translate such a vision into reality will be long, and will require the education and mobilization of new constituencies. This partial list of resources and groups, as well as the suggested activities that follow, offer ideas for further education and action to confront free trade in the Americas.

Educate

Educate yourself, your friends, and your co-workers on the issues. To take on the free trade proponents we have to be able to criticize their arguments and expose the assumptions and narrow interests that disguise the true costs of free trade. We must become more knowledgeable about our continental neighbors, which includes understanding their issues and struggles as well.

- Organize a Discussion-Action project in your workplace, church, school, or community group. Rachael Kamel's *The Global Factory* has some good suggestions and examples. Emphasize the fact that people are challenging and organizing to take control over the decisions that shape their own lives.
- Visit the border area. Groups like the Center for Global Education organize tours to the border areas where you can see first-hand the effects of free trade and learn what local communities are doing to combat it.

• Organize a forum on what the NAFTA means to your community or region. Contact groups like the Fair Trade Campaign, Institute for Food and Development Policy, or the Mobilization on Development, Trade, Labor, and the Environment for speakers.

• Subscribe to periodicals like *The Other Side of Mexico*, and the *Pro-Canada Dossier* which are excellent resources about contemporary political, economic, and social issues and about the movements working to confront free trade.

Advocate

Make your views known to your elected representatives, and demand that they respond by opening up the debate on free trade. Write letters to the editor demanding articles on how free trade will affect your area. Get your union, church, or community group to organize a letter-writing campaign on the NAFTA.

• Write your legislators. Demand that they get the Bush Administration to investigate the real costs of a NAFTA and who will pay them. Demand that they put pressure on the Administration to implement the international labor rights provisions in US foreign trade legislation.

• Write to the corporations who have plants in the maquiladora region. Demand that they comply with the Maquiladora Standards of Conduct developed by the Coalition for Justice in the Maquiladoras.

• Contact the Federation for Industrial Retention and Renewal to talk with people who are doing work on plant closures issues. Support consumer boycotts such as the one organized by the *Trabajadores Desplazados*, a group of workers laid-off when the Green Giant plant transferred work to Irapuato, Mexico.

• Visit your local public broadcasting affiliate and local-access cable channel and help them produce shows on the NAFTA.

• Contact Americas Watch, Amnesty International, the National Network for Immigrant and Refugee Rights and other groups working to end human rights violations in North America. Find out how you can help.

Organize

The struggle to create a North America rooted in a vision that places jobs and justice, food and freedom, development and democracy at its center is a long-term one. The power we have to effect change is multiplied when we act together. Coalitions of environment, labor, consumer, development, and social justice groups have already forced governments to respond to some of the concerns of grassroots organizations. We need to keep the pressure on in examining the impact of the Administration's proposals, as well as articulating our alternatives. We may lose some battles, but the futures of our communities are too important to leave to corporate boardrooms.

- Join your local Coalition for Fair Trade, and get your union or church, to endorse it. If one doesn't exist, organize your own.
- Contact various organizations listed in the resources section to see how you can support their work.
- Organize exchanges between activists in your area and those in Canada and Mexico.

Resources

There are hundreds of books, articles, and other materials which address the issues raised by the NAFTA. The footnotes provide a good start for resources. What follows is just a partial listing of other materials:

Books

Maude Barlow and Bruce Campbell, *Take Back The Nation* (Toronto: KeyPorter Books, 1991).

Walden Bello, *Brave New Third World* (San Francisco: Food First, 1988).

Dan La Botz, *A Strangling Embrace: State Suppression of Labor Rights in Mexico* (Washington, DC: ILRERF, 1991).

Duncan Cameron, ed., *The Free Trade Papers* (Toronto: Lorimer, 1986).

———, *The Free Trade Deal* (Toronto: Lorimer, 1988).

Max Cameron and Ricardo Grinspun, eds., *The Political Economy of a North American Free Trade Area* (St. Martins Press, forthcoming).

Marjorie Cohen, *Free Trade and the Future of Women's Work: Manufacturing and Service Industries* (Toronto: Garamond, 1987).

Joe Foweraker and Ann L. Craig, eds, *Popular Movements and Political Change in Mexico* (Boulder and London: Lynne Rienner, 1990).

Maria Patricia Fernández-Kelly, *For We are Sold, I and My People: Women and Industry in Mexico's Frontier* (Albany: SUNY Press, 1983).

Bennett Harrison and Barry Bluestone, *The Great U-Turn: Corporate Restructuring and the Polarizing of America* (New York: Basic Books, 1988).

Michael C. Mayer and William L. Sherman, *The Course of Mexican History* (New York and Oxford: Oxford University Press, 1983).

Robert A. Pastor and Jorge Castañeda, *Limits to Friendship: The United States and Mexico* (New York: Knopf, 1988).

John Warnock, *Free Trade and the New Right Agenda* (Vancouver: New Star Books, 1988).

Periodicals

The Other Side of Mexico provides news, interviews and analysis of Mexico's popular movements. It is published six times a year in English and Spanish. Subscriptions are $10 in Latin America, $15 in North America and Europe for individuals, $18 and $20 for institutions from Equipo Pueblo, A.P. 27-467, 06760 Mexico, D.F. Checks payable to Carlos A. Heredia/Equipo Pueblo.

Action Canada Dossier (previously the *Pro-Canada Dossier*) is published by the Action Canada Network, 904-251 Laurier Avenue West, Ottawa, Ontario, Canada K1P 5J6. Subscriptions are $25 for individuals, $45 for institutions.

The Ecologist is a bimonthly journal of environmental issues. Annual subscriptions are $30 individual, $65 institutional, and $25 student/retired with a copy of ID. Contact *The Ecologist*, MIT Press Journals, 55 Hayward Street, Cambridge, MA 02142-9949 USA.

Report on the Americas is published five times per year by the North American Congress on Latin America (NACLA). Annual subscriptions are $22 individual, $40 institutional in the US. $32 individual, $50 institutional in Canada, Mexico and elsewhere. Contact *Report on the Americas*, 475 Riverside Drive, #454, New York, NY 10115 USA.

Labor Notes is a monthly news bulletin on developments in the US and international labor movements. Subscriptions are $10 individual, $20 institutional from Labor Education and Research Project, 7435 Michigan Avenue, Detroit, MI 48210 USA Tel: 313-842-6262.

The Multinational Monitor is a monthly that covers corporations and international economic issues. Subscriptions are $22 individual, $25 nonprofit, $35 institutional. For Canada and Mexico add $10 for postage, other international subscribers add $15. P.O. Box 19405, Washington, DC 20036 USA.

Fuera de Línea is a quarterly published jointly by the Partido Revolucionario de las y los Trabajadores and Solidarity, in both English and Spanish. Subscriptions are $7 annually in the US and Mexico and $15 elsewhere from *Fuera de Línea*, PO Box 86479, San Diego, CA 92138 USA.

CrossRoads is a monthly journal of contemporary political analysis and left dialogue. Annual subscription is $24 individual, $40 institutional in the US. Canada, Mexico, Central America, and the Caribbean are $30. All other international $40. *CrossRoads*, PO Box 2809, Oakland, CA 94609 USA.

Z Magazine is an independent political magazine of critical thinking on political, cultural, social, and economic life in the US. Subscriptions are $25 in the US, $50 international, $35 libraries and institutions, $18 low income. 116 St. Botolph Street, Boston, MA 02115-9979 USA.

Special Issues

"Solidarity Across Borders: US Labor in a Global Economy," is a special issue of *Labor Research Review* (#13, Volume VIII No. 1, Spring 1989) published by the Midwest Center for Labor Research, 3411 West Diversey Avenue, Suite 10, Chicago, IL 60647 USA Tel: 312-278-5418.

"Everybody's Business: A People's Guide to Economic Development," is a special edition of *Southern Exposure* 14, nos.5-6, published by the Institute for Southern Studies, 604 West Chapel Street, Durham, NC 27701, USA Tel: 919-688-8167.

"Mexico: Whose Crisis, Whose Future?" (Volume 21, Nos 5-6, September-December 1987) and "The New Gospel: North American Free Trade," (Volume 24, No. 4, May 1991) are special issues of NACLA's *Report on the Americas*.

"The Global Economy: Unions, Workers, Borders," (No 12 July-August 1991) is a special issue of *CrossRoads*.

"Post-Nationalist Mexico and the Latinization of America," is a special issue of *New Perspectives Quarterly* (Winter 1991).

Pamphlets

Maquiladoras and Toxics: The Hidden Costs of Production South of the Border Leslie Kochan. Explores the toxic threat to both Mexican and US workers posed by the proliferation of *maquiladoras*. Available from the AFL-CIO, 815 16th Street, NW, Washington, DC 20006.

Competition or Solidarity: Union Choices in the Face of Free Trade This 80-page booklet for union and community-labor activists includes an analysis of what free trade will mean for workers and a discussion of the ongoing organizing efforts in the three countries. Available in early January 1992 from Labor Notes.

Videos

$4 A Day? No Way! (1991)
A 20 minute video on efforts by Mexican workers to win justice and democracy, and on their growing ties with U.S. and Canadian workers to defend common interests. Contact: American Labor Education Center, 2000 P Street, NW, Room 300, Washington, DC 20036 Tel: 202-828-5170.

Dirty Business: Food Exports to the United States. (1990)
A fifteen minute video, produced by the Migrant Media council, which looks at the potential problems of a U.S.-Mexico free trade agreement. Contact: Migrant Media Productions, PO Box 2048, Freedom, CA 95019 USA.

Global Assembly Line (1983)
An hour-long film which shows how U.S. corporations have moved to countries like Mexico and the Philippines searching for cheap, mostly female labor. Contact: New Day Films, 853 Broadway, Room 1210, New York, NY 10003, USA Tel: 212-477-4604.

Trading Our Future? (1990)
This twenty minute video by the Fair Trade Campaign and League of Rural Voters covers the history and current debates taking place in the General Agreement on Tariffs and Trade (GATT) negotiations. Contact the Fair Trade Campaign, address below.

Organizations

Action Canada Network
904-251 Laurier Avenue West
Ottawa, Ontario
K1P 5J6 Canada
Tel: 613-233-1764
Fax: 613-233-1458
The Network is an umbrella group of national organizations that led the struggle against the Canada-US Free Trade Agreement, and is working to ensure that Canada's future is shaped by and for people, not profits.

American Friends Service Committee
1501 Cherry Street
Philadelphia, PA 19102 USA
Tel: 215-241-7000
Fax: 215-864-0104
contact: Primitivo Rodríguez
The Maquiladora Project has full-time staff in the border region; the Border Project documents and protests human rights violations against Mexicans on both sides of the border.

Association of Farmworker Opportunity Programs
408 Seventh Street, SE
Washington, DC 20003 USA

Tel: 202-543-3443
Fax: 202-546-2331
contact: Lori Rottenberg
This national federation of organizations provides farmworkers with employment, job training, and support services. It is also tracking the NAFTA to analyze its effects on farmworkers.

Canadian Centre for Policy Alternatives
904-251 Laurier Avenue West
Ottawa, Ontario
K1P 5J6 Canada
Tel: 613-563-1341
Fax: 613-233-1458
The Centre produces research reports, books, and other publications and organizes public symposia and conferences on a range of public policy issues. The Centre has published numerous studies of the US-Canada FTA and is currently monitoring the NAFTA. Write for a list of resources.

Center for Ethics and Economic Policy
2512 9th Street, #3
Berkeley, CA 94710 USA
Tel: 510-549-9931
Fax: 510-549-9995
contacts: Ellen Teneinty, Ron Steiff
The Center provides popular economic education training for unions, religious organizations, and community groups who are beginning to understand what it means to live in a global economy. The trainings cover how to apply values and economic analysis to change policies on issues of trade, international investment, employment, standard of living, global debt, and taxes.

Center for Global Education
Augsburg College
731 21st Avenue South
Minneapolis, MN 55454 USA
Tel: 612-330-1159
contact: Sara Nelson-Pallmeyer
The center offers travel seminars in Mexico and throughout Latin America, including perspectives of the poor and disenfranchised as well as the views of decision-makers.

Coalition for Fair Trade and Social Justice
c/o Plant Closures Project
518 17th St.
Oakland, CA 94612 USA
Tel: 510-763-6584
A coalition of labor, environmental, Mexican, church, agricultural, international, and immigrant rights groups working for fair trade agreements and relationships that foster sustainable development and protect workers, communities, and the environment.

Coalition for Justice in the Maquiladoras
475 Riverside Drive, Room 566
New York, NY 10115 USA
Tel: 212-870-2295
Calls on corporations to follow "Maquiladora Standards of Conduct" which are guidelines for addressing environmental contamination, unsafe working conditions, violations of workers' rights, and inadequate public services in border cities. Coalition members have introduced shareholder resolutions at corporate annual meetings calling for respect for these standards.

Common Frontiers
11 Madison Avenue
Toronto, Ontario
M5R 2S2 Canada
Tel: 416-921-7847
Fax: 416-924-5356
contact: Ken Traynor
Monitors the ongoing agenda and process of North American economic integration between Mexico, Canada, the USA and rest of the hemisphere. Facilitates contact and exchanges of people and strategies between Canadian, Mexican and US organizations.

Community Nutrition Institute
2001 S Street, N.W., Suite 530
Washington, DC 20009 USA
Tel: 202-462-4700
Fax: 202-462-5241
contact: Eric Christensen
CNI has been monitoring the impact of the proposed NAFTA on food safety, consumer protection, and environmental standards. They have produced several reports on these issues.

Federation for Industrial Retention and Renewal
3411 W. Diversey Avenue #10
Chicago IL 60647 USA
FIRR is a national coalition of organizations fighting plant closings in the US.

Friends of the Earth
218 D Street, SE
Washington, DC 20003 USA
Tel: 202-544-2600
Fax: 202-543-4710

contact:Alex Hittle
or
4512 University Way, N.E.
Seattle, WA 98105 USA
Tel: 206-633-1661
Fax: 206-633-1935
contact: Andrea Durbin
Friends of the Earth monitors the environmental effects of free trade and produces reports on the issue.

The Development Group for Alternative Policies
1400 I Street , NW Suite 520
Washington, DC 20005 USA
Tel: 202-898-1566
contact: Karen Hansen-Kuhn
The Development Gap organizes forums, facilitates the flow of information, and works with policymakers to help promote a democratic process through which a broad range of views on the FTA, particularly those emanating from popular organizations in Mexico, can be widely heard.

Fair Trade Campaign
Box 80066
Minneapolis, MN 55408 USA
Tel: 415-826-5030 West Coast Office
Tel: 612-379-5965 Midwest Office
A national coalition of labor, farm, church, and environmental organizations working to insure that all trade agreements promote the interests of people and the environment, in the U.S. and around the world.

Institute for Agriculture and Trade Policy
1313 5th Street SE, Suite 303
Minneapolis, MN 55414 USA
Tel: 612-379-5980
Fax: 612-379-5982
contact: Mark Ritchie
Research, analysis, and public education on international trade issues. Write for a list of publications on free trade.

Institute for Food and Development Policy (Food First)
145 Ninth St.
San Francisco, CA 94103 USA
Tel: 415-864-8555
Fax: 415-864-3909
contact: John Gershman
Food First is a research, analysis, and education-for-action center that exposes the social costs of orthodox development strategies and proposes alternative visions for participatory, equitable, and sustainable development.

Institute for Local Self-Reliance
2425 18th Street, NW
Washington, DC 20009 USA
Tel: 202-232-4108
Fax: 202-332-0463
contact: David Morris
Founded in 1974, the Institute researches the potential for reducing the dependence of economies on long distance trade in physical commodities. It also works with governments, businesses, and community organizations who are interested in developing policies and programs to encourage internally generated development. Having provided technical assitance to community-based develop-ment projects in more than three dozen US cities, the Institute has also produced over 20 technical publications.

Institute for Policy Studies
Working Group on the World Economy
1601 Connecticut Avenue, NW
Washington, DC 20009 USA
Tel: 202-234-9382
Fax: 202-387-7915
contact: John Cavanagh
The Working Group analyzes the changing trends in the global economy and its impact on workers, communities, and the environment.

International Labor Rights Education and Research Fund (ILRERF)
100 Maryland Avenue, NE Box 74
Washington, DC 20002 USA
Tel: 202-544-7198
Fax: 202-543-5999
contact: Pharis Harvey
Serves as an information clearinghouse for national organizations concerned that U.S.-Mexico-Canada free trade negotiations will ignore environmental, labor rights, and farmers' concerns. Also conducted a study of labor rights violations in Mexico.

International Union of Food and Allied Workers' Associations
1875 Connecticut Avenue,
NW Suite 708
Washington, DC 20009 USA
Tel: 202-265-4440
Fax: 202-265-0684
contact: Joy Ann Grune
IUF in North America encourages inter-

national communication among unions in different countries on free trade issues, particularly via the international trade secretariats.

Labor Notes
7435 Michigan Avenue
Detroit, MI 48210 USA
Tel: 313-842-6262
contact: Mary McGinn
Labor Notes publishes a bi-monthly by the same name that looks at rank and file union issues, including the NAFTA. They work with union and community-activists to build a national grassroots labor solidarity coalition in the US.

Mexican Action Network on Free Trade
c/o Frente Auténtico del Trabajo
Calle Godard 20
Colonia Guadelupe Victoria
Mexico, D.F.
07790 Mexico
Tel: (52-5) 556-9375
Fax: (52-5) 556-9316
contact: Bertha Lujan
A network of independent and democratic labor organizations, environmental and women's groups, and research and education centers.

Mexico-U.S. Diálogos
870 President Street
Brooklyn, NY 11215 USA
Tel: 718-230-3628
Fax: 718-399-0312
contact: David Brooks
Mexico-U.S. Diálogos, works to promote a binational dialogue based upon the interests of working people in both coun-
ties. Diálogos coordinates binational conferences, seminars, speaking tours, and media projects.

Mobilization on Development, Trade, Labor, and the Environment
Box 74, 100 Maryland Avenue, NE
Washington, DC 20002 USA
Tel: 202-544-7198
contact: Pharis Harvey
MODTLE is a national network of organizations concerned with highlighting potentially adverse effects of a NAFTA and working with Canadian and Mexican groups to work toward alternative proposals.

Mujer a Mujer/Woman to Woman
A.P. 24-553
Colonia Roma
Mexico D.F.
06701 Mexico
or
PO Box 12322
San Antonio, TX 78212 USA
A collective of Mexican, US, Canadian and Caribbean women based in Mexico promoting communication, exchange, and strategic connecting among activist women throughout the region. They publish a newsletter, Correspondencia in both English and Spanish.

La Mujer Obrera
1113 East Yandell
El Paso, TX 79902 USA
Tel: 915-533-9710
La Mujer Obrera works with women garment workers, educating them about their rights as workers and advocating fair wages, safe working conditions, and an end to sweatshops.

National Network for Immigrant and Refugee Rights
310 8th Street
Oakland, CA 94607 USA
Tel: 510-465-1984
contact: Arnoldo García
The Network is an education, advocacy, and resource center working for immigrant and refugee rights.

National Wildlife Federation
1400 16th Street, NW
Washington, DC 20036 USA
Tel: 202-797-6603
Fax: 202-797-5486
contacts: Ted Stimpson, Stewart Hudson
The National Wildlife Federation is the nation's largest conservation organization. The Federation works to educate individuals and organizations to conserve natural resources, to protect the environment, and to build a globally sustainable future.

Public Citizen
215 Pennsylvania Avenue, SE
Washington, DC 20003 USA
Tel: 202-546-4996
Fax: 202-547-7392
contact: Lori Wallach
Public Citizen works to democratize the trade negotiating process, and to insure that trade between nations does not threaten consumer health and safety nor the environment.

The Resource Center
Box 4506

Alburquerque, NM 87196 USA
Tel: 505-842-8288
contact: Debra Preusch
The Resource Center highlights and analyzes the connections between U.S. foreign policy and women, labor movements, the environment, and native people. They will be producing Mexico: A Country Guide, *for release in late 1991 and a book on U.S. influence in Mexico in 1992.*

South and Meso American Indian Information Center (SAIIC)
PO Box 28703
Oakland, CA 94604 USA
Tel: 415-834-4263
Fax: 415-834-4264
contact: Karl Guevara Erb
SAIIC's goals are to promote peace and social justice for Indian Peoples. SAIIC is embarking on further research on the impact of the NAFTA on Indigenous people in Mexico, as well as Central and South America.

Texas Center for Policy Studies
1800 Guadalupe, Suite B
Austin, TX 78701 USA
Tel: 512-474-0811
The Center is a policy research and advocacy organization that works with environmental and community groups in Texas and northern Mexico.

About Food First

The Institute for Food and Development Policy, popularly known as Food First, is a non-profit research and educational center focussing on issues of food and democracy around the world. Founded in 1975 by Frances Moore Lappé, author of *Diet for a Small Planet*, and Joseph Collins, the Institute has worked to change accepted views on the causes of, and solutions to, world hunger. More recently the Institute has been actively promoting the vision of participatory, equitable and ecologically sustainable development in the Third World.

Nearly all our income comes from our members and from sales of our books. We accept no contributions from government sources. Our research is independent, free from ideological formulas and prevailing government policies. Members receive a free book for joining, a 25 percent discount on books and the quarterly *Food First News* and *Action Alerts*.

Other Food First books of related interest

A Fate Worse than Debt: The World Financial Crisis and the Poor
Susan George's fascinating work on the world debt crisis and its effect on the poor. The author of *How the Other Half Dies* uncovers the human side of debt: the countless poor whose lives are destroyed to bail out banks and bankers. Yet, as George reveals, the crisis could be an opportunity to transform Third World debt from an instrument of starvation, oppression, and misery into one of productivity, democracy, and hope. $8.95 paperback

Brave New Third World? Strategies for Survival in the Global Economy (Development Report 5)
Walden Bello asks if Third World countries can finish the next decade as vibrant societies? Or will they be even more firmly in the grip of underdevelopment? The outcome, Bello argues, depends on their ability to adopt a program of democratic development which would place them on a more equal footing in the global economy. $6.00 paperback

To order books, receive a free catalog or to join Food First please write:
The Institute for Food and Development Policy
145 Ninth Street
San Francisco, California 94103, USA
Tel. 415-864-8555
or charge your order or membership: Call 1-800-888-3314

The Institute for Policy Studies

For nearly thirty years, the Institute for Policy Studies has been a leading center for progressive scholarship and activism. Its public scholars start from the premise that ideas are vital to social and political change and they work with a range of citizen movements to analyze key problems and chart alternative policies and paths forward. The Institute's free trade work is part of a larger set of inquiries and educational products on the impact of globalization on development strategies around the world. For more information write or call:

The Institute for Policy Studies
1601 Connecticut Avenue NW
Washington, DC 20009 USA
Tel: 202-234-9382
Fax: 202-387-7915